ANDERSONVILLE TO TAHITI

The Amazing Story of Dorence Atwater

THOMAS P. LOWRY

Andersonville to Tahiti

TABLE OF CONTENTS

ACKNOWLEDGEMENTS

Beverly A. Lowry, wife, companion, and co-researcher, located and summarized the trials of Dorence Atwater and Henry Wirz, and translated during our taxi-borne search for Atwater's Tahiti gravesite. Rev. Dr. Albert H. Ledoux contributed his research on the Florence prison and translated difficult French documents. M. Antoine Kher made additional clarifications of *la belle langue Française.* Our initial decade in the National Archives owes an unending debt to Michael P. Musick. DeAnne Blanton has continued his manifold good works.

Mrs. Louise L. Stange, of the Plymouth Historical Society, provided great help with Dorence Atwater's hometown history. Bill Armstrong surprised me with the Pennsylvania death lists. Robert E. L. Krick was my authority for Belle Isle prison and all Richmond questions, while Robert K. Krick shone his light upon Civil War Virginia in general. Richard S. Lowry, Jr., helped with ship identification. F. Terry Hambrecht, MD researched the Confederate doctors. Melvin Smith found the funeral photos in the Connecticut State Library. Liz Argentieri of SUNY Geneseo provided the image of the aging Dorence Atwater.

In Tahiti, I received generous assistance from M. Gerard A. Cowan, M. Fernand de Loos, M. Jimmy Ly, Mme. Kaiwa Metzker, Mme. Véronique Mu-Liepmann, and Mme. Agnès Tchoung Yao.

And special thanks to my great-grandfather, Pvt. William H. Simms, 1st Michigan Engineers & Mechanics, for not dying at Andersonville. If he had, I never would have existed.

For those I may have forgotten, I offer my thanks and my apologies. As in all such endeavors, any errors or omissions remain mine.

PROLOGUE

He is dying. At ten in the evening, the greatest artery in his body suddenly burst. For days, he had felt the strange and terrifying stirrings in his chest as little fibers stretched and tore. Then, like the final breaching of a fatally flawed dam, the wall of his aorta gave way. In a moment of agony and fading consciousness, he was suspended between life and death.

As his body crumpled to the floor at San Francisco's Hotel Normandie, Dorence Atwater's life flashed before his eyes: the harsh New England winters of his boyhood home, the screams and explosions of a dozen Civil War battles, the hunger pangs at four Confederate prisoner of war camps, the refulgent moment of freedom, his hidden documents which brought resolution to 20,000 grieving parents, the degradation of fresh imprisonment, imposed by the very government he had fought for, and, stranger than any dream, his final decades by the blue waters and jungle flowers of a tropical paradise, with his lovely bride by his side – a Polynesian princess, no less – and his mature years of wealth, honors, and long-delayed appreciation.

A few more seconds and blood no longer flowed to his heart and to his brain. He was, in fact, dead. His spirit left him, rising swiftly above the chill sea breeze of the Golden Gate, into the darkest blue of the sky, coursing east across America, circling briefly over the red clay of Georgia, where his own country had betrayed him, then in a flash over the chill walls of New York's Albany Prison, the site of a betrayal even more bitter, gathering speed as the veteran's phantom crossed the Atlantic, traversed central Africa, and paused briefly off the coast of Somalia, his temporary island home, then on to hover above a lush green Tahiti plantation. Its earthly circuit done, the path was upward, upward into that plane whence no man has yet returned.

Still, the story is not all told. Dorence, the hero of Andersonville, had been betrayed twice by his own government, but now it would be his widow's turn. Perhaps recalling Abraham Lincoln's Second Inaugural Address – "…to care for him who shall have borne the battle, and for his widow, and for his orphan…" – she applied for a widow's pension. In a carnival of obtuse obstruction, bureaucratic delay, compulsive search for negative evidence, and sheer pig-headed refusal to see the obvious, her request was delayed not for months, but for years. The investigation cost, no doubt, more than the small pension that she was finally awarded. In the end, she, like her late husband, triumphed. And in the final act of a drama that literally united the ends of the earth, she entered that condition where no clerk or auditor could reach her. Death.

This then will be our story, the sadly forgotten tale of a man whose courage and good deeds were punished, whose life was finally saved by the founder of the American Red Cross, whose starved, sickly, and abused body would soon be joined in marriage to a real life princess. A life almost beyond imagining, a life begun in the constrained and rigid atmosphere of a New England village, in the very heart of the Victorian era, and ending in a culture whose traditional dances, with their frenzied drumming and wild hip gyrations, shocked generations of Christian missionaries. A life whose nadir was a hole dug in the Georgia clay, a hole which would have brought shame to a self-respecting gopher, and whose zenith found our hero dressed in the finest tailored clothing, dining with his royal family, and receiving visitors such as Robert Louis Stevenson.

Thrice betrayed. Thrice triumphant. A life worth knowing. A tale worth telling.

CHAPTER 1

Out of the Mists of Time

Do we really know the traverse of Atwater's spirit as it left his body that night in San Francisco? Of course not. It was a metaphor, a flight of fancy on the author's part, an act of poetry, not a committing of history.

But we do have a storehouse, a veritable plethora, of real Atwater data, primary sources, original documents – all the sorts of things that make a story credible. Not myth, not tradition, not fanciful creations of later revisionist historians, not an attempt to tear down or build up the stature of our central character, but rather an effort to make the documents speak for themselves.

Where did Dorence come from? The practice of genealogy has fascinated some and bored others to tears. The almost impenetrable genealogies in the first book of Chronicles, chapters 6 & 7 and the begats in Matthew 1: 1-16 are equally dense. They will try the patience of the most dedicated reader. Why should Atwater's forebears be any more interesting? Because they serve to show his deep roots in the twin villages of Plymouth and Terryville, there in the heart of Connecticut. Dorence was not just off the boat, trying to comprehend what it is to be an American. He was not like millions of Californians today, who are from somewhere else. Dorence was firmly planted in one spot. Dorence's great great-grandfather, Samuel Atwater, fought the redcoats in the American Revolution. Samuel's son Timothy settled in Plymouth around 1780 and married Lydia Humiston. They produced Wyllys Atwater, who married Fanny Purdy. Wyllys sired Henry, by now the third generation of Plymouth-Terryville Atwaters. And Henry married Catherine Fenn. Be patient; our genealogical excursion is nearly completed. Henry and Catherine produced Dorence, our protagonist.

Along with Dorence, there were four siblings who play little part in our story: Theresa, Eugene, Catherine, and Richard. Dorence's third brother, Francis, an author and publisher, was his staunchest defender, and fought for the good name of Dorence even when Dorence was long dead.

Death came not just to Dorence. His mother died in 1863, while her son was serving in the Union Army. His father died in 1865, just as his sickly and emaciated son returned home. For the Atwaters, the war had no happy ending, and even then there was worse to come.

And what of these twin villages during the Civil War? For most of us alive today, the military is something we see on television. Our armed forces are very small in relationship to our huge population. The men and women who are dying in the mideast are someone else's sons and daughters, not ours. (Not entirely true; the author's son is a US Marine Corps officer.) The war is abstract, far away, a painless war. It doesn't even cost money; somehow, almost miraculously, we have cut taxes, not increased them.

In the 1860s, the armies of the North totaled almost 2.5 million men, enormous in proportion to the size of the nation back then. Disease and bullets killed nearly 600,000 men, counting both North and South. And in the heart of the Constitution State the leading citizens put their own lives on the line, not just someone else's life. Col. Augustus Fenn had his arm shot off at Cedar Creek and was back on duty in seven weeks. Major William Ells was crippled at Cold Harbor. Lt. Horace Hubbard was killed at Opequan Creek. Life in the ranks was no easier. Burritt Tolles died of fever and was buried at Terryville. Charles Cleveland died of fever and was buried at Terryville. George Holt died of diphtheria and was buried at Terryville. Franklin Hubbard died of typhoid and was buried at Terryville. George Hoyt died of fever and was buried at Plymouth. Eben Norton died of fever and was buried at Plymouth.

The profession of embalming expanded greatly during the war. "Embalming surgeons" followed the armies and became skilled at pickling the shattered corpses, shipping the loved ones home for burial, usually in a zinc-lined box, which kept the body fluids from leaking into the wooden floor of the baggage car.

At Cold Harbor, Philo Fenn was shot in the head and John Murphy was shot in the heart. George Beach had his thigh torn open by a shell fragment and died. James Baldwin died in a Confederate prison. At Petersburg, John Grieder, Charles Guernsey, and George Hempstead were shot and killed. At Opequan, Hiram Coley, Franklin Candee, and Horace Hubbard all died. More died at Fisher's Hill and at Cedar Creek. All these deaths were from two small villages. The list of wounded is far longer: shattered arms, shattered legs, and shattered faces, endless and incurable and often fatal cases of diarrhea, and many men weakened by malaria. Dozens were deaf from the cannon's roar. Many had screaming nightmares, reliving sights that no man should ever see. Somehow, inexplicably, some returned to health and lived full lives. Why was one man ruined by the war and another man not? Who is to say? Fate is the hunter. Always.

It should be painfully clear that this war was not shiny medals, waving banners, and handsome uniforms. It was a fiery furnace, a meat grinder. Every citizen of Plymouth and Terryville knew that. And, like so many of his fellow citizens, Dorence Atwater stepped forward, stepped forward to defend his beloved Union.

CHAPTER 2

From Enlistment to Capture

During the Civil War, most Army units were state regiments. The regular Army, the "old Army" of the frontier forts, was a tiny fraction of the Union forces. Recruiting for the state regiments was mainly the responsibility of the state governors. Most regiments carried names such as the 3rd Iowa Volunteer Infantry or the 4th New York Heavy Artillery. The large states fielded the largest number of regiments. New York sent out 194 regiments of infantry, plus numerous units of cavalry and artillery. Connecticut fielded 29 white infantry regiments plus one regiment of "colored troops."

Dorence Atwater enlisted in the Connecticut Squadron of Cavalry on August 21, 1861 at Hartford, Connecticut. Army records say that he was eighteen years old; birth records say that he was sixteen. He stood 5'8" tall, had blue eyes and light brown hair. His occupation? Clerk. A month later his Connecticut Squadron was consolidated with selected units from New Jersey, Indiana, Vermont, and New York, to form the 2nd New York Cavalry, also known as the Harris Light Cavalry.

Dorence's regiment saw plenty of action. They were rushed into service because of the fear of Confederate invasion, and on September 18, 1861 left New York State for Washington, DC, even before they had finished their formal organization. At first they were part of McDowell's Division of the Army of the Potomac; over the years they were attached to several different brigades and divisions.

In March 1862 they left the defenses of Washington, DC and advanced on Manassas, from whence, in April, they went on to Falmouth., and spent much of the time, May through July, at

Fredericksburg, Bowling Green Road, and Flipper's Orchard. In late July they formed part of expedition to Hanover Junction, and then went on a reconnaissance to James City. August 1862 found them at many spots: Hall Station, Thornburg, Orange Court House, and on the 9th day, at the Battle of Cedar Mountain. After Cedar Mountain, they covered a lot of ground before September rolled around: Rapidan Station, Brandy Station, Fords of the Rappahannock, Kelly's Ford, Catlett's Station, Culpeper, Waterloo Bridge, Sulphur Springs, Manassas Junction, Thoroughfare Gap, Groveton, Bull Run, Germantown, and Chantilly. They were at Little River Turnpike as September opened and two weeks later were at South Mountain. They saw action at Leesburg on September 17th ; ten days later they continued their tour of northern Virginia at Warrenton. Moving swiftly east, they arrived at Dumfries on the Potomac River by the fifth of October. From there, they filled their October calendar with visits to Hazel River, Aldie, and Mountsville. Still criss-crossing northern Virginia, the Harris Light Cavalry occupied themselves in November with visits to Sudley Church, New Baltimore, Warrenton, Upperville, Rappahannock Station, and back to Aldie. December began with a quick warm-up to the massive Battle of Fredericksburg by a scuffle at Stafford Court House. December 12th through the 15th were the fateful days in which Maj. Gen. Ambrose Burnside bloodied his own army by feckless uphill attacks, creating 12,000 Union casualties.

Among those killed were two of the author's great great-uncles. Michael Conrad Lowry, 39th Pennsylvania Volunteers, whose body was never identified, and John Suhrie, 133rd Pennsylvania Volunteers, who was shot in the chest, died in a Georgetown hospital, and is buried, under the name "Jno Shure." in the Soldier's Home Cemetery on the heights overlooking Washington, DC.

At the time of Fredericksburg, Atwater's cavalrymen were part of the brigade of Brig. Gen. George D. Bayard, an 1856 graduate of West Point. In 1860, a Kiowa arrow imbedded itself in his upper maxillary bone. The wound never healed properly and in 1862 he took a two week leave of absence from his command of the 1st Pennsylvania Cavalry. The surgeons opened up the middle of his face and drained the pus from a large abscess. Eight months later, he was off duty for fourteen days with a bladder infection. As the infantry fighting raged at Fredericksburg, Bayard was sitting in his tent near the Barnard House, on Burnside's far left, well back from the action, awaiting orders. His health took a turn for the worse when a stray cannon ball ripped through his thigh. Within hours, he bled to death, in spite of the surgeon's best efforts. The 2nd New York Cavalry saw no action and suffered no casualties that day.

Atwater's unit saw little action for the next four months. Most armies were in winter camp and it seems likely that the men, horses, and equipment were all in need of rest and repair. What a year of adjustment 1862 was for Dorence! Unlike the Southern boys who spent much pre-war time on horseback, and the Confederate officers who brought their own horses and engaged in sports like riding to the hounds, Dorence as a sixteen-year store clerk of modest means may never have been on horseback, much less spend his leisure time in equestrian events.

The regiment's combat year of 1863 began at Rappahannock Station on April 14, 1863, and zigzagged across northern Virginia for the next two months. Then Robert E. Lee's invasion of Pennsylvania began. Atwater and his regiment headed northeast and were in Rockville, Maryland, on June 28. Two huge armies were headed for the little town of Gettysburg. In February 1863, Dorence had been assigned duty as a clerk (he had excellent handwriting) on the staff of Col. Judson Kilpatrick. On the 4th of July 1863 (other records say July 2 or July 7) Dorence was carrying messages to Kilpatrick's headquarters when fate caught up with him. Near Hagerstown, Maryland, two Confederates, wearing Union uniforms, captured him and sent him to the Confederate prison on Belle Isle in the James River near Richmond.

The war continued without him and the Harris Light Cavalry was there to the bitter end, the signing of the surrender at Appomattox. By the close of hostilities, the regiment had lost 112 enlisted men and one officer to mortal wounds, and 235 enlisted men and one officer to disease. Their troubles were over; Dorence's troubles had just begun.

CHAPTER 3

A Guest of the Confederacy

Two weeks after his capture, Atwater arrived at Belle Isle prison camp. It's probable that he walked the entire way. In the course of the Confederate invasion of Pennsylvania, roughly 5,000 Union men were captured. Lee's retreating army traveled mostly on foot, with wagons for supplies and for the wounded. Where there were railroads, the increasingly broken down Southern trains were also reserved for wounded men and vital supplies. It is easy to imagine 5,000 defeated and hungry men trudging the 190 miles towards an unknown fate at the hands of their captors. We do know now that over 30,000 Union soldiers died in Confederate prisons. As the boys in blue went south, did they know that many would never return?

Belle Isle Prison was on an island in the middle of Virginia's James River, very close to Richmond, the capital of the Confederacy. There, on six acres, lived over 9,000 prisoners of war. In the summer the heat and humidity were oppressive and the stench of unwashed bodies and poor sewage facilities must have been dreadful. The winters were cold enough to freeze the surrounding river. One of the most vivid descriptions of life at Belle Isle was recorded in the diary of Quartermaster Sgt. John Ransom of the 9th Michigan Cavalry, who arrived at Belle Isle in November 1863, where he stayed until moved to Andersonville in March 1864. Here are a few high points of Ransom's diary as recorded at Belle Isle.

"Food but once a day...very cold...at least 100 men limping with frozen feet...all men forced to stand in the freezing rain [for no reason] all day, barefoot...by evening six could not walk and three had died [of hypothermia]...a man deranged with fever and half naked walked up the [off-limits] steps and was shot through the head...river frozen...rebel officers sent to hand out clothes do so very slowly to make the job last as long as possible...socks knit in the North have romantic notes in them...hundreds with frozen feet, ears, hands...scurvy and smallpox are here...sutler is selling cheese for $10 a pound [$300 in today's money, if the $10 was Federal money]...Sanitary Commission food sent for prisoners is making rebel officers fat...rebel officers all drunk during the holidays...one man bucked and gagged for stealing sour [spoiled] beans from the swill barrel...20 more men died last night...Lt. [Virginius] Bossieux's dog was stolen and eaten by Yank prisoners...he is very mad...men reduced to almost skeletons." Such was Dorence's introduction to Confederate prison life. (By the way, in various records, he appears as Dorance, Dorrance, Dherence and Hatwater.)

Belle Isle

Civil War photos of Belle Isle are rare and of poor quality. This one shows tents and the James River in the distance. In the right foreground, the man on the right with the shiny cap, dressed all in black is Lieut. Virginius Bossieux (Co. F, 25th Battalion, Virginia Infantry) whose dog was eaten by starving Union prisoners.

In November 1863, Atwater was transferred to a different prison, Smith's Tobacco Factory, on the west side of 21st St. between Main and Cary Street in downtown Richmond. The factory was taken over by the Confederate government when the war began and was for a time General Hospital No. 17. Its prison population was about one-tenth that of Belle Isle. There at the old tobacco factory Dorence was put in charge of supplies sent from the North for the use of Union soldiers, a useful application of the skills he had learned as a clerk in a store in his hometown of Terryville. His careful attention to inventory resulted in the discharge of one Confederate officer who had been stealing items addressed to Union prisoners.

On the front page of the Richmond *Sentinel*, on December 30th 1863, appeared a brief and apparently innocuous item, which, looking back, was the first warning of an impending tragedy. Were the words of that newspaper meant to be ironic or was the writer actually sincere? Either way, he had this to say. "Change of base—it will not be long ere many of the Yankee prisoners now in confinement on Belle Isle will have an opportunity of breathing the salubrious air farther south, the government having made selection of a spot in Georgia near Andersonville, Sumter County, for their reception and safekeeping, their present place of confinement being rather overcrowded. The [new] location is on the Southwestern Railroad, where no difficulty will be encountered in supplying their wants." Salubrious? Safekeeping? No difficulty...in supplying? It sounds almost like a vacation travel brochure. This apparent luxury resort opened for business in February 1864.

Ordinarily it would not have concerned Dorence. He was safely indoors at the tobacco factory, inventorying clothing, not at Belle

Isle. The jailors at Belle Isle were ordered to assemble several batches of exactly 400 prisoners and shepherd them to the train depot, to be shipped to Andersonville. One night, a batch of Belle Isle prisoners were being marched to the waiting cars when the rebel officers noted that they were a few men short of the required 400. Dorence was roused out of his bed, half asleep, and marched off with the others, headed for his rendezvous with destiny.

The heavily-guarded train rattled its way south, averaging ten miles-per-hour over the Confederacy's increasingly dilapidated rail system, with its worn and wheezing locomotives. Transportation in the South had for years been slowed by a particularly feckless manifestation of local rights. Each railway company decided on the spacing of its rails. While most agreed on a standard gauge, when a train reached a competing line that had different concepts of rail spacing it was likely to find rails to narrow or too wide for the axles of the approaching train. Teamsters were employed to unload, by hand, the contents of one train and convey those goods to a waiting train a few yards away. The United States did not settle on a universal standard gauge (56.5 inches) until 1900.

As Dorence's Andersonville-bound train traveled south through Virginia, North Carolina, South Carolina, and Georgia it is likely that its passengers changed trains more than once. Finally, they pulled to a stop at the last depot. For many men, it would be "the end of the line" in every sense of the word. The newly arrived prisoners marched through opened gates into a sixteen-acre enclosure surrounded by a sixteen-foot-high stockade fence of freshly hewn pine logs. At thirty-yard intervals these stockade walls were topped with sentry boxes, each occupied by a Confederate soldier, fully armed. Nineteen feet in from the tall stockade wall was a low, crude fence, the "dead line." Any man who crossed that line was shot. There were no trees. There were no buildings. There was no form of shelter of any sort. There was no protection from the scorching sun of the Georgia summer nor from the cold winds and rain of the Georgia winter. As the months passed, the prisoners managed to acquire a random assortment of pup tents, scraps of canvas, and blankets, which provided some minimal shelter.

The only water supply was a branch of Sweetwater Creek, called Stockade Branch. In a remarkable feat of Confederate engineering, one which would have puzzled the Roman aqueduct engineers, outside the stockade and upstream from the prison, Confederate authorities had placed the camp of the Confederate guards, the horse stables, the dead house where corpses were kept, and the bakery. This almost guaranteed that the water supply, even as it entered the stockade, was polluted. At first, there were no organized latrine facilities within the stockade, so each man lived in a hole filled with feces and urine washed down the slopes with each rainstorm. It would be no surprise to learn that diarrhea was common among the prisoners, as they drank the excreta of every man upstream and uphill.

As to nutrition, the Belle Isle men arrived half starved and were soon on their way to being fully starved. Consider corn-on-the-cob. We all know to eat the soft kernels but not the hard cob, which is durable enough to be made into corncob pipes. The provisions at Andersonville included cornmeal which had been made by grinding up dried corn, kernels and cob. For generations, Southern housewives had been buying this sort of cornmeal which they sifted through a porous fabric called "bolting cloth." This removed the sharp cob granules while preserving the nutritious cornmeal. There was no bolting cloth at Andersonville. The cob fragments not only had no nutritional value but were almost as abrasive as ground glass. Men's intestines, lacerated by cob particles and poisoned by the disgusting and infectious water supply, were rarely without painful and debilitating bowel symptoms.

In June 1864 the stockade area was enlarged to enclose an additional ten acres. This was hardly enough to relieve the terrible crowding. Soon the prison reached its maximum number of inmates—32,000, or 1,230 men per acre. An acre is a square 209 feet on each side. Not all the space was habitable. The area near the creek was a swamp of noxious sewage. Several areas were so steep that a weakened soldier might fall from his tiny "home." Dozens of prisoner-dug wells provided water, but were also night-time death traps. Each man had a personal area a little smaller than a king-size mattress. This patch of dirt was his bed, his living room, his kitchen, and often his toilet. If he burrowed into the ground to seek some shelter from the sun he had only a sharp stick or his hands to build the new shelter (a few lucky men had spoons or half-canteens) and with every rainstorm his hole would fill with filthy muck.

The Confederate army, with its chaotic railroad system, its distribution of goods based on wealth and social class, and it's backwards industrial base, could not provide enough shoes. As soon as a Union soldier was taken prisoner, he was likely to find his shoes on his captor. The Georgia soil was famous for hookworms (*Necator americanus*), which delight in entering bare feet. Soon the bloodsucking worms joined *E. coli* and the cob fragments in assaulting the prisoner's intestines.

Although the Georgia climate was ideal for growing vegetables, with their essential vitamins, no such effort was made for the prisoners. Farmers raised only what they needed for their families. The Confederate government entered into no contracts which might have motivated vegetable production. Scurvy was the inevitable result. New wounds would not heal, old wounds opened up again. Pellagra was a scourge of poor Southerners within living memory. It is a disease of niacin deficiency and a product of bad diet. Its many symptoms include diarrhea. It was with diarrhea that

Dorence was admitted to the prison hospital on May 18, 1864. Going to the hospital was not to be taken lightly. For many men, the next step was the dead house, where they briefly stored corpses before burial. Prisoners tried to avoid the hospital and the doctors did not need any additional patients. Today when we think of "hospital," we think of gleaming corridors, air-conditioning, elevated beds, nurses in starched uniforms, bright lights, and stainless steel food carts. The Andersonville hospital was several acres of bare dirt, surrounded by a crude fence. A motley assortment of rotted tents covered some of the patients. Others just lay in the sun or the rain. A fortunate few had a blanket or some pine needles as a mattress. The "nurses" were other Union soldiers, who often abused or stole from the helpless men jammed together on the ground. A Confederate report stated that half the doctors were incompetent. There were often no medicines at all. Nearly everyone was covered with lice. Dorence must have been very sick indeed to go to the hospital.

However, his diarrhea was not only his curse but also his salvation. After a month of treatment, and perhaps better nutrition, he was improved. Someone had noticed his fine penmanship and he was assigned to work as a clerk in the office of the surgeon Dr. I. H. White.

Isaiah H. White was born in Accomack County, Virginia in 1838 and received his degree from the Medical College of Virginia in Richmond in 1861, the same year that the war began. In 1862 the Confederate Senate confirmed his commission, with the rank of assistant surgeon. Over the next two years he served at the enormous Chimborazo Hospital in the suburbs of Richmond and with the 14th Louisiana Infantry. White was on duty at Macon, Georgia in February 1864 when he was appointed chief surgeon at Andersonville prison. He was age twenty-six and now had responsibility for the health of 30,000 starving men. White was regarded as competent and hard-working, doing his best with very limited facilities, but he was hardly sympathetic to the Union's cause. In May 1863, the 1ˢᵗ Regiment of United States Colored Troops was organized. In 1861 the Vice President of the Confederate States had said, "Our new government's foundations are laid, its cornerstone rests, upon the great truth that the Negro is not equal to the white man, that slavery...is his natural and normal condition." A soldier is a human being; a slave is property, not fully human. (The original U.S. Constitution agreed.) A black soldier was a contradiction in Southern eyes and the Confederacy responded with an edict that captured black soldiers would be put into slavery and that their white officers were to be shot. Maj. Archibald Bogle, of the 1ˢᵗ North Carolina Colored Infantry, had been badly wounded and captured at Olustee, Florida. Officers were usually sent to separate prisons, but Bogle went to the main stockade at Andersonville, an all-enlisted facility. When he appeared at Dr. White's hospital to have his wound attended, he was ejected with, "Put him out with his Niggers!" Post-war, Dr. White practiced thirty years in Richmond and died in 1907.

At the hospital Dorence's new job was to keep a daily record of the deaths of Union prisoners. This might not seem like a busy task, but the prisoners were now dying at an average rate of fifty men per day. And buried just as rapidly, to prevent the spread of disease and to reduce the horrible order of fifty rotting corpses putrefying in the hot Georgia sun, corpses already covered with swarms of flies laying their eggs in the liquefying flesh, eggs which in just a few days would become legions of crawling, squirming maggots.

For each dead soldier, Atwater recorded: Grave site location number, last name, first initial, regiment, company, date of death, and cause of death. Dorence had to work fast—one case every six minutes. Dorence had to work fast—his comrades' corpses were decomposing even as his pen scratched furiously across the paper. In addition to the daily record, he was also to make monthly and quarterly abstracts.

Did this excellent work on behalf of his captors give him the opportunity sleep in the hospital? Not at all. Each evening at sundown he was passed back through the gates, back into the stockade, to sleep in his little hole in the ground amidst the stench, filth, and noise of 30,000 angry, desperate, and dying men.

When he began his job of keeping the dead list, he was told that when the war was over the list would be given to the Union government. Atwater's desk was next to that of camp commander, Capt. Henry Wirz, and the young prisoner was no fool. He quickly noted that records were poorly kept and that business was conducted in a casual and slipshod manner. This not only offended the efficient and organized mind of the New Englander, but it also suggested that the death list was unlikely to ever reach the North. That would mean that many thousands of families would never know what happened to their son or to their father.

Atwater decided to make a duplicate list in secret. This meant he had to not only work twice as fast as usual, with only three minutes per entry, but also to conceal the second list from Wirz who sat only a few feet away. Dorence concealed his copy of the list in the lining of his coat and escaped detection hundreds of times as he passed through the closely watched gates each morning and each evening.

Those of you who have attended burials or seen them on television will have seen that there is one grave for one coffin. At Andersonville there was no lumber for coffins nor time to build them if there had been lumber. There were no individual graves. There was a trench six feet wide, four feet deep, and roughly 100 feet long.

Each day approximately fifty men were dumped into the trench and packed tightly side-by-side. There were no fat corpses, though some are already bloating from the gases of putrefaction. (We don't know if Dorence attended these mass burials as part of his record keeping.) Roughly twelve inches apart, crudely numbered sticks marked the last resting place of each Union soldier. When one ghastly trench was full, another trench was dug and the whole process repeated. When the war was over and the last living Union soldier began his journey home, he left behind 12,914 comrades rotting beneath the soil of Georgia.

Such shocking mortality—29% of all prisoners, and 39% if you count the men who died while being transported to other prisons—surely meant that something was very wrong and if it was so wrong, who was at fault? Such a question merits its own separate chapter.

Dorence worked at his hidden list from mid-June 1864 to late September 1864. He must have found ways of adding the names of men who had died in the three months before he began keeping the record, since his final list was remarkably complete. On September 2, 1864 William Tecumseh Sherman's army entered Atlanta and would soon begin its famous march to the sea. A huge Union army was in the very heart of the Confederacy.

An issue often overlooked is the fact that Dorence was probably not even a soldier during the last six months of his imprisonment. He originally enlisted for three years on August 29, 1861, in the 1st Squadron of Connecticut Cavalry. That unit was folded into the 2nd New York Cavalry two days later. Most soldiers who enlisted after July of 1861 were enrolled for three years. The optimistic days of early 1861 included ninety-day enlistments, which proved far too short.

By mid-1863, Federal authorities were looking forward with dread to the summer and fall of the following year, when the terms of all these three-year men would expire. Something had to be done to keep the armies from collapsing. The men had to be convinced to re-enlist ahead of time. With morale in the regiments still fairly high, and with a bonus and a furlough dangled in front of the soldier's eyes for added motivation, a majority of Federal servicemen were in fact persuaded to re-enlist in the fall of 1863, many months before the expiration of their terms. Since Dorence Atwater had been in captivity since July of 1863, it is fairly certain that he was never given the opportunity to re-enlist. His Compiled Military Service Record makes no mention of a re-enlistment. We can say with a high level of certitude that Dorence ceased being a United States soldier on August 29, 1864.

It is not exactly clear, 150 years later, why the Confederate authorities feared the release of the 30,000 prisoners at Andersonville. Most of them were so shattered by scurvy, diarrhea, malnutrition, and malaria that they could never return to military service. Thousands could not even walk. Did the South fear condemnation for the condition of the men? Did they wish to keep them as pawns in the ongoing chess game of prisoner exchange? This explanation is a plausible one; as long as Lincoln and Grant kept Rebel prisoners locked up in the North, the Confederates only hope of ever redeeming them lay in keeping hold of the Yankee prisoners. If Sherman freed them, the Southern bargaining chip was gone. Did they fear that these crippled multitudes would somehow swarm over the Deep South, wreaking revenge with rapine and murder? Not likely. Whatever the motivation, the Confederate government began the enormous and urgent task of relocating the Andersonville men away from Sherman's path,

Large numbers of Andersonville prisoners were put on the move, some to prison camps in South Carolina and others to prisons near the coast of Georgia. In September 1864 Dorence Atwater was one of those men. His route north and the timing of his transfer are unknown. Charleston, South Carolina was a likely waypoint. He was in Florence, South Carolina, a new hellhole, anywhere between three and five months. A Confederate scribe at Florence recorded him as Dhorence Hatwater, but the regiment and company designation leave no doubt that this is our Dorence.

NO.	NAMES IN ALPHABETICAL ORDER. (*By Regiments and Companies.*)	RAN
✓	Ramsdell Osnaldo, 4	4
✓	Maltby Dexter, 6	
✓	Hyde Solon	Hos
✓	Hatwater Dhrence	P
✓	Cutting Andrew	Ca
✓	Smith William H,	V
✓	Bush John	
✓	Dugan Patrick	
✓	Smigtleton Thomas	
✓	Park Thomas	
✓	Edson George W.	
✓	Bone E. W	C

The first evidence of Dorence Atwater's stay at the Florence prison was found by Albert H. Ledoux on this roster. Atwater's misspelled name is on the fourth row from the top. The rest of his entry reads, "Pvt. Co. D, 2 NY Cav, captured July 7, 1863, Hagerstown," which confirmed the identity.

While nearly forgotten for more than a century, the Florence facility has recently seen a revival of interest, with research, publications, and commemorations. The Florence prison opened in September 1864 and closed in February 1865. Like at Andersonville, the graves were marked by numbered stakes, but the burial and hospital records did not survive. The National Cemetery at Florence has nearly 2,800 tombstones marked "unknown." The area where groups of dead were thrown in common graves has no stone markers at all.

The post commanders, Col. George P. Harrison, Jr., 32nd Georgia, Maj. Frederick Warley, South Carolina Artillery, and Lieut. Col. John Iverson, 5th Georgia, were known for their fair treatment; on the other hand Lieut. James Barrett, 5th Georgia, who commanded the interior of the prison, was noted for his viciousness and brutality, and during its brief existence Florence was worse than Andersonville. When the war was over Barrett fled immediately to Germany where he remained for many years.

Roughly 18,000 Union soldiers spent time at Florence, of whom 2,800 died. It also had little or no shelter and a desperately inadequate supply of food. Once again, Dorence survived Confederate captivity without his list being discovered.

Near the end of February 1865, after a resumption of prisoner exchanges, Dorence found himself among several thousand Florence internees sent to Wilmington for handover to Federal authorities. Wilmington was the last Atlantic port still open to Confederate traffic and sustained a long siege, holding out until February 22, 1865. With the consent of Gen. U. S. Grant in Virginia, the paroled Union sick and wounded men were essentially being sent to what was still a combat zone.

Union Maj. Gen. John Schofield, who was in charge of the siege, was reluctant to call off his attack to take charge of thousands of prisoners, however lamentable their condition. He furthermore asserted that he had no orders to do so, in spite of the fact that Gen. Grant had already issued those orders days before. Faced once more with the possibility that their prisoners would eventually be taken by force, Confederate authorities shunted them inland to Goldsboro to wait for the general to change his mind. A repetition of Grant's orders achieved the desired effect. Brought back down the track from Goldsboro, the men were formally handed over at the site of a destroyed railroad bridge, the "Northeast Bridge," so named because it spanned the northeast branch of the Cape Fear River inland from Wilmington.

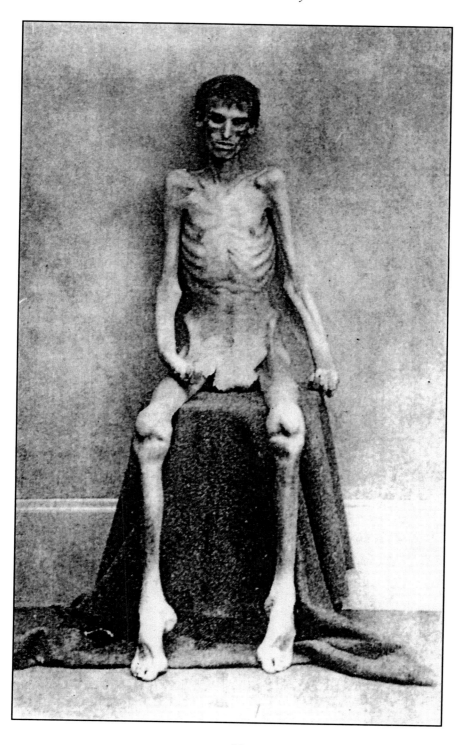

This desperately malnourished Union soldier was typical of thousands of men who came north out of Confederate prison camps. Many never regained their health.

Soon the streets, barns, and houses of Wilmington filled with dazed, emaciated men who had been starved for months, then shuttled north and south, fifty men to a box car, unwanted by either their captors or by the Union commanders. It took almost a month for Union transport ships to collect all the former prisoners at Wilmington. Dorence's exact journey is unknown but we do know that he was paroled at "N.E. Ferry, N.C." (the same locale as the Northeast Bridge) on December 28, 1865. His exchange roll has the dual date February 27/28, 1865, probably indicating that his group came across the lines late one day and early the next. He reported at College Green Barracks, Camp Parole, Maryland, on March 10, 1865. He was finally back in the Union. One ordeal was over. Another was about to begin.

CHAPTER 4

Who Was to Blame?

Before we pass on to the next phase of Dorence's life, let us ponder that question. Something dreadful happened at Andersonville. How did it happen? Who was responsible? Were Union prisons any better?

First, what about deaths outside the prison? According to Frederick H. Dyer's *Compendium* 2,778,304 men served in the Union Army. Of these 110,070 (3.96%) were mortally wounded and 199,720 (7.19%) died of disease. Just joining the Army and never even seeing a battle brought a 7.19% mortality, but even a relatively safe Confederate prison, such as the one at Florence had a death rate of 16%, more than double the "normal" Army mortality.

The two largest prisons were Andersonville with 45,000 passing through and a 29% death rate and the Union facility at Camp Douglas, Illinois with a total of 30,000 prisoners and a 13% death rate. Clearly, Andersonville was worse than Camp Douglas.

At the local level, there was much confusion at Andersonville because of the somewhat irrational command structure. First, there was the post commander, usually Brig. Gen. John Winder, then there was the commander of the troops guarding the prisoners, and finally there was the commander of the prison itself, Capt. Henry A. Wirz. Dr. White was in charge of medical care. When all of these men cooperated, things ran relatively smoothly, which was rare. Quarrels over precedent, jurisdiction, rank, date of rank, and of type of commission, were frequent.

The next steps up the bureaucratic chain were the commissary officers. If one of the commanders at the prison ordered some needed item it had to be approved at various levels up to and including people in the nation's capital, Richmond. Even when all the approvals had been signed, the item might be unavailable, or the price had changed.

The local farmers preferred not to sell at the price fixed by the Confederate government; they got more for their products on the open market. The rapid devaluation of Confederate currency only increased the merchant's incentive to avoid supplying the prison.

An example of the difficulties in building such a facility was the shortage of nails. The stockade itself was made by putting logs vertically into a trench. Slaves and strict supervision of the slaves were all that was necessary. But the massive gates needed nails. Commercial nails were almost impossible to find. Rural Georgia had not entered the Industrial Age. Locally made nails were created, one by one, by a blacksmith with a hammer.

The author has read much of Wirz' correspondence with his superiors. He was well aware that the prison was shockingly overcrowded, that there was no shelter, that the food supply was inadequate. He asked for more of everything. He supported the efforts of the prisoners when they acted to control the criminal element in the prison population. He built structures to reduce pollution in the water of Stockade Branch. He genuinely wished to provide better care. His work was made no easier by an unhealed compound fracture of his right forearm. There was a gaping wound, where the rotting ends of the bones could be seen, oozing pus. His surgeon offered to treat it but Wirz feared, not unreasonably, that the treatment might be worse than the disease. He simply wrapped his arm in a towel and continued to work.

The end of the war produced jubilation in the North, accompanied by a wish for revenge, a demand for punishment. The assassination of Lincoln, widely believed to be a plot of the Confederate government, turned much of the jubilation to bitterness. The sudden influx of returning prisoners, mere wasted skeletons, many more dead than alive, stoked the calls for vengeance. (The author's great-grandfather, William H. Simms, left no written record of his Andersonville experience.)

Jefferson Davis was in prison, awaiting a trial that never happened. John Wilkes Booth died at Garrett's barn. Gen. John Winder escaped the whirlwind by falling dead during an inspection tour of the Florence prison. That left Wirz, who was arrested and swiftly brought to Washington, D.C., where he was tried for war crimes in a trial presided over by Maj. Gen. Lew Wallace.

Wallace was the hero of the Battle of Monocacy and soon to be the author of *Ben Hur – A Life of the Christ*. But at Wirz' trial, Wallace was neither heroic nor Christ-like. The trial was a farce, a travesty, a kangaroo court. Wallace excluded witnesses who were favorable to the defendant and coached the prosecution witnesses in a carnival of fraud, perjury, and fabrication. The court was intended to hang and hang him they did. This shocking miscarriage of justice ended on November 10, 1865 as his body dropped six feet and the hangman's noose snapped his neck. His wife, who had not been allowed to visit him during the trial was also not allowed to have his body. The politicians and yellow rag journalists had bayed for blood, someone's blood. With Wirz' death their fury lessened.

The Northern prisons were no pleasure palaces. Elmira had a 24% death rate; the grim reaper took 13% at Camp Douglas. This system also had its villain, Maj. Gen. William Hoffman, very much an old Army man. He had been appointed Union Commissary General of Prisoners. He had the mind of an accountant out of a Charles Dickens novel. He followed the letter of the law but not the spirit. His books always balanced. Like in the South, there were shortages of everything and where there was room for discretion, Hoffman erred on the side of the penurious.

Another vital factor in prisoners' suffering was the subject of exchange and parole. Early in the war, prisoners were "exchanged," one man for one man, and both were free to resume fighting. Later, as the numbers swelled beyond the captors' ability to feed and confine them, prisoners were "paroled," i.e., they gave their word to abstain from taking up arms until formally exchanged. The paroled men either went home to await orders, or to a designated parole camp. In the Spring of 1863, the system began to break down over two issues. The Confederacy announced that captured US colored troops would be executed or sold into slavery. The North replied that no Confederate prisoner in a Union camp would go home until black soldiers were treated as whites. The second issue was the 30,000 Confederates captured at Vicksburg. William T. Sherman paroled them; the South unilaterally declared these men "exchanged," and they were soon back killing Yankees. By 1864, all exchanges had halted and the prisons of both sides swelled far above capacity. There is also evidence that Lincoln, Stanton, and Grant recognized that the North could more easily replace lost men than the South, with its smaller population. It can be argued that the cessation of exchange speeded the end of the war and thus saved lives in the long run, but to the men in Andersonville it meant the feeling of being abandoned by their own government, abandoned to die in misery.

But beyond all of the accounting and policy problems lies a deeper question. How do nations get themselves into war with so little reflection on "What comes next?" In the immediate present, we have Iraq, a war started by a small group which ignored the history and sociology of the invaded country. Hitler invaded Russia, certain of victory because of his contempt for the Slavic people. Japan with a small population and no oil, coal, or steel attacked the far larger United States, based on its feelings of Japan's moral superiority. All the leaders of Europe, in 1914, outdid themselves in self delusion about easy victory. In 1897 William Randolph Hearst sent artist Frederick Remington to Cuba to find a war. When Remington telegraphed that there was no war, Hearst shot back, "You furnish the pictures, I will furnish the war." The final result was ten years of bloody fighting with the Moros of the Philippines, America's first contact with Islamic fanatics.

In 1861, newspaper editors north and south denounced each other and promised easy victory. Preachers, north and south, thundered from their pulpits that God hated (or approved of) slavery, and the politicians assured their respective flocks that honor demanded a war. In the race to self deception, the Southern politicians may have been the winners. Armisted L. Burt of South Carolina was so sure that the North would back down that he offered to drink personally all the blood that would be shed by secession. (By 1865, that would total 3 million quarts.)

Dueling as a way of settling questions of honor had faded in the North, but was still a vital element in the chivalry of the Southern upper classes, exactly those men who would form the excellent Confederate officer corps. Honor was everything. Just as North and South both underestimated the scope and cost of the war, both underestimated the challenge of feeding, housing, and clothing hundreds of thousands of prisoners. Gallantry always gets a better press than groceries.

Perhaps Wirz was not a very lovable man, but it does seem an injustice to have him do penance for all the crowing editors, blustering politicians, and thieving merchants, North and South, whose perverted notions of manly virtue, and willingness to cheat their respective nations laid the groundwork for those twenty-six acres of hell at a little train stop in central Georgia.

Dorence arrived in Annapolis on March 10, 1865. His father would die five weeks later. His mother had already died while Dorance was away with the 2nd New York Cavalry. Surely fate had dealt him sufficient grief, but fate was not finished with Dorence Atwater.

CHAPTER 5

Marking the Dead

The next twelve months of Dorence Atwater's life was a tangled tale, with two major threads: the actual marking of the Andersonville graves and the disposition of the dead lists (and of Dorence himself). We begin with the first thread, and three major players: Clara Barton, James H. Wilson, and James M. Moore.

Barton was famous for her work in organizing help for the Union wounded and her later founding of the American Red Cross. There had previously been no tradition of national cemeteries, or of graves registration, much less the sophisticated DNA identification of soldiers' remains that we have today. No Victorian carriage carried bumper stickers with "MIAs never have a nice day." Barton was one of the first to realize the need to locate missing soldiers, and opened an office on 7th Street in Washington, DC, where she began helping families trace their missing loved ones. Among her many honors was the Order of the Red Cross, presented to her in 1902 by the Czar of Russia, recognizing her international contributions to the relief of suffering.

The next player in marking the Andersonville graves was Union Maj. Gen. James H. Wilson, a man strangely overlooked by most history writers. Wilson graduated from West Point in 1860. His engineering skills were vital in the siege of Vicksburg. His versatile talents in organization and combat soon brought him to command all of Sherman's cavalry and even defeated the wily Nathan Bedford Forrest, at Selma, Alabama. From there, Wilson's men swept across the Southeast, capturing not only whole states, but also the death list that Atwater had prepared with the knowledge of Capt. Wirz and Dr. White. That list was still in the hands of the remaining Confederates at Andersonville. What we will call the "Wilson List" had 10,500 names, 2,400 names short of the list that Atwater had smuggled north.

The third player was James M. Moore, who was a captain and assistant quartermaster in the regular Army in 1865. He had begun the war as a private in the 19th Pennsylvania Volunteer Infantry and by 1865 had risen far, receiving not only a regular Army commission and a captaincy, but also a brevet major's oak leaf for "faithful and meritorious service." By 1895, he was a full colonel. His fondness for quartermaster work suggests that he liked "things" better than he liked "people." Barton, whose people skills had given her entrance into the corridors of power went to see Edwin Stanton, Lincoln's crusty, short-tempered Secretary of War. Stanton tolerated neither fools nor frauds. Dorence had shown his list to Clara Barton and they agreed on both the value and the practicality of marking the graves. Stanton listened carefully to Barton; he could see that this idea was neither foolish nor fraudulent, and immediately set in motion Special Orders No. 12 from the Quartermaster General's office, which ordered Capt. Moore, with Barton, Atwater, and three dozen workmen, clerks, and letterers, to go to Andersonville and mark the graves.

On his return, Moore filed a 2,000 word report. It is shocking to find in it no mention of either Clara Barton or Dorence Atwater. Not one word. Moore seems to have deeply resented the presence of a woman on the expedition. (This resentment was not helped by Barton's late arrival at the dock, which delayed the ship's departure.) What he may have disliked about Dorence Atwater is unknown. Moore began his September 20, 1865 report with: "I left Washington on the 8th of July last, with mechanics and materials for the purpose of [marking the graves]." The only name in the entire report is that of Eddy Watts, a "letterer" who died of typhoid. Each grave site had been marked originally by small wooden stakes placed by Union prisoners under Confederate supervision. Moore's expedition had brought 95,000 feet of ten-inch boards, three kegs of nails, 2,600 pounds of white lead for making paint, 500 pounds of "Patent Dryeo", and twenty-five paint brushes. The workers busied themselves leveling the often collapsing burial site, painting the ten-inch boards white, and neatly lettering in name, rank, and unit on each wooden tomb "stone." Moore forbade both Atwater and Barton's participation in this work. Excluded from the grave marking, Clara busied herself as a nurse for the many men coming down with the local illnesses of malaria and typhoid. Dorence, the only member of the party who had actually been a prisoner there, gave guided tours. When the work was complete, Capt. Moore surprised Clara by giving her the honor of raising, for the first time, the Stars and Stripes over the newly marked and landscaped cemetery. The cemetery today takes much the same shape as in 1865. A few empty spaces show where families retrieved their loved ones, but most of the Union dead are right where they were dumped 140 years ago.

Moore's report tells much about conditions in Georgia immediately after the war. The marking expedition sailed south on the steamer *Virginia* on July 8, 1865 and arrived at Savannah, Georgia a few days later. The rail connections from Savannah to Macon were broken. Travel to the prison by wagon was impossible. Sufficient horses were not available and the roads were very bad. Moore spent a week in Savannah, telegraphing Augusta, Atlanta, and Macon almost daily, and always receiving "The railroads are not completed." On July 18, a reply informed him that the Augusta and Macon railroad to Atlanta was now open. The next day the party boarded a riverboat, steamed up the Savannah River to Augusta, and from there was able to travel directly by rail to Andersonville, arriving there July 25, 1865. The rail trip from Augusta to the prison, a direct distance of 120 miles, took six days, an average speed of two miles per hour. The work of grave identification, headboard painting, and landscaping began July 26 and was completed August 16. Moore was assisted by a company of the 4th US Cavalry (part of Wilson's forces) and a company from the 137th US Colored Infantry. Several of the cavalry men died from "fever." This was probably malaria, and many of the men that came with Moore from the North became too sick to work, with illnesses not specified in the report. Moore did not name the dead cavalrymen.

A few miles north and south of Andersonville the soil was good, according to Moore's report, but near the prison it was "sandy, sterile, and unfit for cultivation." The temperature in the shade was 110 degrees. "It is said to be the most unhealthy part of Georgia, and was probably selected as a depot for prisoners on account of this fact." Moore described most of the local inhabitants as from "the most ignorant class...haggard and sallow...from the chills and fever [malaria]."

At Andersonville, during the marking expedition there were two, perhaps three death lists. The first was the "Wilson List," the second was the "Hidden List" that Atwater had concealed in his coat lining while he was in captivity. It is probable that he had with him in addition a copy made of the "Hidden List," which would have constituted a third list.

While the grave marking was in progress, up north in Washington, DC the trial of Capt. Wirz had gotten underway. A messenger from Washington arrived at Atwater's tent and claimed the "Original Copy" (it is unclear what is meant by that) and left Dorence's "Hidden Copy" with him. On August 18, as the grave marking expedition started back to Washington, DC, by way of Chattanooga, Nashville, and Cincinnati, Atwater still had his copy in his trunk and it was still there when the train pulled to a halt in the nation's capital on August 24, 1865.

Dorence had arrived at Camp Parole, newly freed, on March 10, 1865. Now he was back north again on August 24. Five months had passed and the 12,000 grieving families still did not know the fate of their boys in blue, nor had they any idea that these lists even existed. Was the War Department about to relieve their minds? Would Dorence Atwater succeed in having the list published?

The answer lies in that famously cynical proverb, "No good deed goes unpunished."

CHAPTER 6

No Good Deed Goes Unpunished

Dorence Atwater had proved himself in battle, first as a trusted messenger for the highly aggressive Col. Judson Kilpatrick, and secondly in the fight to preserve the names of dying prisoners, by keeping his own secret list and maintaining it intact through the heat and rain of two dreadful imprisonments, and the crowded jostling of a dozen train rides, ending in a sea voyage. Dorence knew the mind of the combat soldier.

Now he encountered a different form of the military mind: the professional administrator, usually holding the title of adjutant. An adjutant is the principal aide to a commanding officer, whether the command be a regiment, a division, or a corps. He is a personnel officer, a record keeper, an organizer of ceremonies, a recorder of hiring and firing, of coming and going.

At the top of the heap is the Adjutant General, the chief military administrator for a president or for a governor. The Adjutant General had many helpers, the AAGs, or assistant adjutant generals. They devoted themselves not only to their work but, in a common human failing, to the jealous preservation of their powers and their little kingdoms. In Atwater's life these traits were embodied in two men, men who would haunt Dorence even beyond the grave.

Samuel Breck graduated from West Point in 1851 and spent ten years as a lieutenant in the artillery service. Perhaps disenchanted with the paralyzingly slow pattern of promotion in his previous branch of service, he became an AAG in 1861 and held that title for the next thirty-six years.

We must digress a moment here to discuss brevet ranks, which are a form of "Thank you, well done." At the end of the war, thousands of officers were given a brevet promotion, usually one rank up. This did not count for additional pay or power, but had a "feel good" quality and enabled many colonels to call themselves "general," and many captains to call themselves "major." There were two common types of brevet commendation: "for gallant and meritorious service," awarded for combat service, and "faithful and meritorious service," for the paper pusher. A sardonic World War II journalist described one administrative officer as "having commanded an LMD." (Light mahogany desk.)

In 1865, having vanquished mounds of paperwork, Samuel Breck was made a brevet brigadier general for "diligent, faithful, and meritorious service in the Adjutant Generals department during the war."

Col. Samuel Breck, assistant adjutant general, was the moving force behind Atwater's Union court-martial and imprisonment. Forty-five years later, he still believed he had done the right thing.

Atwater's other nemesis was Edward Davis Townsend, who completed his West Point studies in 1833, twelve years before Dorence was even born. Townsend had been in adjutant work in the old hidebound Army for decades when the war began, and in 1861 held the ranks of colonel and AAG. At the end of the war, he was brevetted major general for "faithful, meritorious, and distinguished service in the Adjutant Generals department." In 1869 he reached the pinnacle of Army bureaucracy. He became the Adjutant General. Dorence had already had his first brush with the administrative mind, in the form of Assistant Quartermaster Moore, leader of the grave-marking expedition. True, Moore organized and completed his mission successfully, but his petty and small minded maltreatment of Dorence Atwater and Clara Barton revealed a dark side. (It would be wrong to besmirch all administrators. George C. Marshall, Eisenhower's right hand man, was the apotheosis of administrators: wise, innovative, self effacing, and infinitely productive. Sadly Dorence Atwater met no George C. Marshall.)

In 1865 Dorence Atwater had one overriding goal, to publish the list of Andersonville dead, to relieve the minds of thousands of grieving families. In the matter of the death list, it is not clear what formed the goals of brevet generals Breck and Townsend.

When Dorence arrived at Camp Parole in Maryland in March 1865 his term of enlistment had expired seven months earlier. He could not get a furlough—because he was no longer in the army! Accommodating quickly to this bit of bureaucratic madness, he wrote to Secretary of War Stanton, requesting a thirty day furlough, for the purpose of having the death list published. Before an answer came back from Stanton, the commander of Camp Parole issued Dorence a furlough. He went directly to his home in Terryville, Connecticut, where he was sick for three weeks with diphtheria, an often fatal condition with painful festering sores in the throat.

Meanwhile, Samuel Breck had taken an interest in Atwater. On March 13, 1865 he telegraphed Maj. J. A. Haddock at Elmira, New York, "If Dorence Atwater Company D, Second New York Cavalry reports to your office for muster out please furnish him transportation and send him to this office at once bringing the list of soldiers who died in the Rebel prison now in his possession. Acknowledge receipt."

Breck sent two telegrams to the Commanding Officer at Camp Parole. "March 20. Is Dorence Atwater Second New York Cav. at your post. If so has his term of service expired. Answer by telegraph." Four days later, Breck telegraphed again. "Please send Dorence Atwater Company D Second New York Cavalry to this office, bringing the list of soldiers died in Rebel prisons now in his possession as soon as he returns from furlough. Acknowledge receipt." The concept of "possession" loomed large in Breck's thinking.

Dorence was at home on April 12 recuperating from his diphtheria, when Breck telegraphed him ordering him to bring the death rolls to Washington immediately. The next day, despite still being sick, he boarded a train south and arrived in Washington, DC the day of Lincoln's assassination. It was also a day when Breck was out of town. Dorence left the death rolls with Breck's chief clerk. On Breck's return, around April 16, he told Dorence that Stanton had authorized $300 to buy the rolls. Dorence recalled, "I told him I did not wish to sell the rolls, that they ought to be published for the benefit of friends of the dead." Breck replied that Dorence had twenty-four hours to decide whether to take the $300. Since Breck now had all the copies of the rolls, Dorence had little to bargain with, but he did have a counter proposal. "I agree, if I can have a clerkship in the War Department, the $300, and my rolls back after the War Department has copied them." Breck agreed to these terms but added a condition: Dorence must reenlist, this time in General Services, which would place him under the military justice system. Breck now held all the cards. Dorence agreed to the conditions, reenlisted, and was given a furlough home until June 1. (He was still very weak from malnutrition, malaria, and diphtheria.)

In May, while still at home in Terryville, he telegraphed Breck asking if the copying was complete. The answer: "Not yet." In early June Dorence reported for duty as a clerk in the War Department. After six weeks, the rolls were still not copied. Dorence wrote asking if he could copy them at night on his own time. Breck responded, "I have fully explained the matter to General Townsend and he says the rolls shall not be copied for any traffic whatsoever."

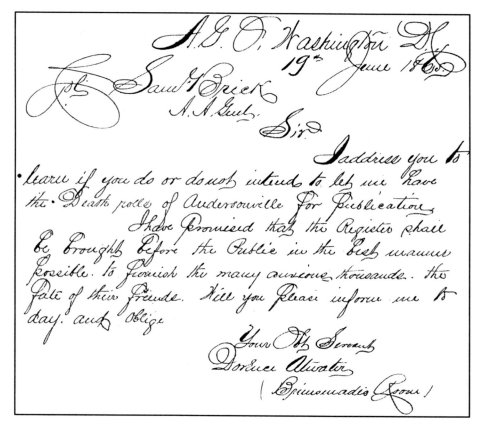

In this hand-written note to Col. Breck, Dorence Atwater demonstrated both the beautiful penmanship that got him a clerk's job at Andersonville and his deep devotion to the families of the Andersonville dead.

By early July when the grave-marking expedition departed, Breck's office had copied Dorence's list. There were now three lists: first the Wilson List, often referred to in the records as the "Original List;" the second was the "Hidden List" made by Dorence and concealed under his coat, and the third copy that was made in the War Department and is called, for the reader's convenience, the "Breck List," which seems to be a copy of the Hidden List. All these were in Dorence's tent at Andersonville, it would seem, when the messenger arrived to collect evidence for the Wirz trial. (Other sources say the lists were in Capt. Moore's tent.) The messenger was given the "Wilson List" and the "Hidden List." Dorence so far as can be ascertained, retained the "Breck List" as per his agreement with Breck. As Dorence later wrote, the Breck List "was mine and lawfully in my possession." On returning to his clerk job in the War Department, Dorence took the precaution of placing the "Breck List" in a "safe place" which he would not reveal. Breck demanded the return of that list as well. Dorence refused, saying that he had a right and a duty to publish the names. Breck's response? "We might as well come to an understanding about these rolls. This is the last conversation you and I will have about them. If you pay back the $300 you can keep the rolls, otherwise you must return them." (Dorence has spent the $300 taking care of his dying father and then burying him, as well as for medication for his many illnesses. There was no Veterans Administration back then or medical benefits for sick veterans.) Dorence reminded Col. Breck of their original agreement. Breck replied that the agreement no longer held, since Atwater "planned to set himself up in business." The discussion became more heated. "I don't consider publishing them for the benefit of the families as 'Setting myself up in business.' I plan to see Secretary Stanton." Breck sent for the guard and had Dorence arrested. He spent the next two nights in the guard house and then was transferred to Old Capitol Prison. It was now late August 1865.

Soon came a court-martial presided over by Lt. Col. Jeffrey Skinner of the 2nd Connecticut Heavy Artillery. Dorence was charged with conduct prejudicial to good order and military discipline, "in that he did unlawfully and without authority seize and take from the tent of Captain James M. Moore, AQM, certain property of the United States…then in the proper charge and custody of the said Captain Moore, to wit a list written upon about 24 sheets of paper of federal prisoners of war who had died at Andersonville, Georgia the same having been prepared by said Atwater while a prisoner at…Andersonville and sold and disposed of by him to the US Government for the sum of …$300 and did appropriate and retain the said property to his own use, this at Andersonville, Georgia 16 August 1865." He was also charged with larceny, the wording of the specifications being identical.

Capt. Moore's clerk testified that there were two lists, the one captured by Wilson's men and the one kept in secret by Dorence Atwater, then the clerk spoke of "duplicate lists." The testimony is very confusing as to which list or lists were on the grave-marking expedition. Other witnesses told the court that after Atwater refused to give up his one copy of the list, that agents had searched his room at the United States Hotel on Pennsylvania Avenue. This witness said that only when they could not find the list in Atwater's hotel that he was locked up. The witness did make it clear that the missing list was a copy of the list that Atwater had smuggled north in his coat lining, and that the government had already had the original list and had no need to pay for them. What the government had paid for was the <u>copy</u> which did not belong to Atwater. In brief, the prosecution's case asserted that Atwater had never been entitled to any of the copies of any of the lists at any time, not even the one he had made in secret and had hidden in his coat through three prison camps.

Col. Breck told the court that Atwater had demanded more than the $300 authorized by Secretary Stanton and had wanted to keep a copy on top of that. "I told him that we had the power to take the lists from him. I informed him that he could not have copies of his list." Then Breck added that he had no knowledge of who had which list, then remarked further that the lists were not indispensable, "because we had taken from the rolls the data necessary for the transaction of business." What he meant by that is quite unclear.

Breck went on. "I told him, give back the $300 and you can keep the rolls," and added that he was "disgusted" by Atwater's belief that he was entitled to any copy of the rolls. Breck concluded with a most puzzling statement, which is paraphrased here; "The War Department has not made a copy of the rolls. We have not had the time."

Next up was Capt. Moore, organizer of the grave-marking expedition. "I was detailed to go to Andersonville with a number of mechanics...also to take care of Miss Barton, who accompanied me as a guest, and to notify Mr. Atwater, now a clerk in the War Department to accompany me." Moore said that he traveled with two lists: the Wilson List captured from the Confederates and a copy of Atwater's original list, a copy given directly to Moore by Col. Breck. This was the copy "that Atwater had made himself and is the copy that is missing." Which list was which became more obscure with each witness.

But Moore's next statement added further to the confusion. "The roll that is missing is the roll taken by the accused [which] was copied from the original rolls captured by General Wilson."

Sebastian Balway, a clerk in the Death & Disability room of the Adjutant Generals office, was asked if they had prepared the Anderson death lists for general distribution. "We wrote circulars to the company commanders to inform them of the death of the men and from these circulars we made a memorandum. The memoranda are kept in our offices on file. They are part of our records."

Atwater's defense counsel prepared a thirty page rebuttal which concluded, "To him and to him alone the War Department and the country are indebted for the full names and numbers of the graves of the prisoners who died at Andersonville. The records captured by General Wilson are imperfect, lacking 2,000 names."

After brief deliberation, the court found Atwater guilty of both charges. He was sentenced to a dishonorable discharge, a fine of $300, and eighteen months in prison at hard labor. Further, he must stay in prison until he repaid the original $300 and returned the death list that he had hidden from Col. Breck.

The sentence was approved without comment by Maj. Gen. C. C. Augur and by Judge Advocate General Joseph Holt. As a captain at Old Capitol Prison prepared Dorence for his trip to the prison at Auburn, New York, he told the guards, "I want that Atwater handcuffed damned tight; I know what kind of a fellow he is; I have heard of him before." Under guard and in irons, Dorence was marched through the streets of Washington, DC to the Baltimore & Ohio railroad station.

Several things are remarkable about this court-martial. First, Atwater's recall of the events and the testimony of the prosecution witnesses agree hardly at all. Someone was lying or misinformed. The government witnesses seemed to disagree with themselves and with the other government witnesses. The definitions of the various lists of Andersonville dead are confusing and contradictory.

What seems most remarkable is that no War Department person seems to have had the slightest intention of making the lists available to the American public, much less to the anxious parents and spouses of missing prisoners.

This episode closes with Dorence Atwater beginning a long prison sentence at hard labor, hard labor for a body seriously underweight and sick with a least two diseases. The death list that he had so lovingly prepared was still locked away in the War Department, (with an additional copy at an unknown location) outside the awareness of any of the family members that had a loved one under that sandy Georgia soil.

CHAPTER 7

From Prison to the Indian Ocean

The late Autumn of 1865 found Dorence Atwater facing eighteen months — or more, if he failed to conjure up the $300 while breaking rocks behind prison walls — in the dank confines of Auburn prison, yet two years later, tropical trade winds brushed his cheek on a little scattering of islands far off the coast of Kenya. How came about his freedom, plus a comfortable salary, 10,000 miles from Washington, D.C.? That is a tale in itself.

Yet we must divert for a moment into a little known facet of the Andersonville story. It would appear that Col. Breck would go to any extreme to prevent the publication of the Andersonville rolls, yet a large fraction of them had already been published! On Saturday evening April 15, 1865, the Pittsburgh (Pennsylvania) *Evening Chronicle* published the grave numbers, names, and regiments of every Pennsylvania soldier who had died at Andersonville.

The newspaper editor's explanation raises as many questions as it answers. "AN IMPORTANT RECORD. Complete list of deaths, regiment, company and number of the graves of all the Pennsylvania soldiers in the Andersonville, Georgia prison from February 24, 1864, to March 24, 1865 compiled from the official records of the prison expressly for the Evening Chronicle. We, today, present our readers with a complete record of the deaths of Pennsylvania soldiers in the Andersonville, Georgia prison, compiled by Charles M. Colvin, of Company E, 1st Excelsior Regiment [70th New York] who was confined in that delectable hole over 15 months, and was during the greater portion of the time employed as a clerk in the hospital. It should be carefully preserved for future reference by those having friends buried in that locality as it will enable them, in case they desire to bring the bodies home, to find them without trouble." Following this editorial note is column after column, page after page, of the list of dead men, organized by the month of death.

Were Colvin and Atwater both working at the Andersonville hospital and hiding duplicate copies, unknown to each other? Or were each keeping a list in case one was caught the other would have a back-up copy? The Pittsburgh list was Pennsylvania soldiers but Colvin was a New Yorker. State rivalries were intense; why would a New Yorker research Pennsylvanians? Was the Pittsburgh list overlooked by Col. Breck because it came out the day of Lincoln's assassination? All unknown. What we do know is that Colvin survived the war and died in Morris County, New Jersey on August 7, 1904 of "organic heart trouble, resulting from pneumonia."

Atwater was in prison, but his friends were not, and they included Clara Barton, Gen. Benjamin Butler, Horace Greeley, editor of the New York *Tribune*, and host of Connecticut politicians, all incensed that a local boy was in prison for what seemed a nonsense. After two months in prison, an order signed by Stanton released Dorence. He was not pardoned. His guilty verdict was not overturned. He was not discharged by the order of any court. He was just — out. On November 30, 1865 he was suddenly a free man. Officially, he was still guilty, but he was physically free and he set to using that freedom.

He retrieved his copy (the Breck copy?) of the "Hidden List" from where it had been concealed and set to work preparing it for publication. After forty days and forty nights of incessant labor, the work was done. In late January, 1866, Horace Greeley published the complete death list — over 12,000 names. The special edition, more like a book, sold for twenty-five cents. Atwater received not one penny for his work; Horace Greeley sold the list at cost. The publication found buyers as fast as it came off the presses. The published list contained not only the names of the dead, but also a long introduction by Dorence and an even longer essay by Clara Barton. Her concluding words are worth repeating.

"A mere report, unaccompanied by the 'record,' seemed but a hollow mockery, which I would not impose upon you, and this is my first opportunity for such accompaniment. For the record of your dead, you are indebted to the forethought, courage, and perseverance of Dorence Atwater, a young man not yet twenty-one years of age; an orphan; four years a soldier; one-tenth part of his life a prisoner, with broken health and ruined hopes, he seeks to present to your acceptance the sad gift he has in store for you; and, grateful for the opportunity, I hasten to place beside it this humble report, whose only merit is its truthfulness, and beg you to accept it in the spirit of kindness in which it is offered."

Atwater's Magnum Opus was done. Now, he applied himself to clearing his name. On the 22nd of March, 1866, he sent his memorial to Congress, detailing his long journey from prison in Georgia and beyond, asking for inquiry and justice. New York Congressman Robert S. Hale reviewed the evidence and declared to the House of Representatives: "I say, on my reputation as a lawyer and as a man, that it is impossible for any intelligent man to read the record of that court-martial without saying it is a case of the grossest and most monstrous cruelty and injustice that ever oppressed any human being."

Hale sent the case to President Andrew Johnson for review. Johnson, in turn, sent it on to Judge Advocate General Joseph Holt, who responded on May 10, 1866 in a long report which concluded with a maddeningly excessive use of the passive voice, "What is now desired appears to be that the stigma resting on Atwater's character, arising from a conviction of felony be removed. It is suggested that no formal pardon has yet been issued to him, he having been released from confinement by an order of the War Department. A pardon may therefore be issued to him, setting forth the grounds on which it is granted, to-wit, the insufficiency of the testimony on which his conviction rested. This, it is believed, would afford as impressive an evidence of the president's judgment and would as effectually remedy the discredit which has attached to Atwater as would an attempted annulment of his conviction and sentence."

Adjutant General Townsend, who had pushed the trial and conviction of Atwater, objected strongly to Holt's recommendation of a pardon. "Such an act of clemency...would give a coloring to his (Atwater's) false representation against the Adjutant General's office." The president, caught between two advisors, did nothing. He gave the case to Stanton — who did nothing.

Before the civil service system, federal jobs were doled out in an enormous, complex, and informal network of favoritism, the so-called spoils system. If the administration was Republican, Federal jobs went to Republicans. The same for Democrats and their supporters. Life for Dorence Atwater was moving on; it was now summer of 1866 and the country had other fish to fry: Reconstruction, the Freedman's Bureau, restarting the state governments of the Confederacy, pardons for Confederate politicians. Atwater's friends wanted to get him a government job, preferably one out of sight.

In the 1860s, the federal government was still small enough for nearly every employee to be fitted into one thick book, *The United States Official Register*. In the 1867 volume, we find "Dorence Atwater, consul, Seychelles, compensation 1,500." The date is puzzling, because the State Department's records show, "The president of the United States of America...reposing special trust in...Dorence Atwater of Connecticut...do appoint him consul at Seychelles...and enjoin all captains, masters, and commanders of ships...armed or unarmed...to acknowledge him accordingly... and do request Her Britannic Majesty...to peacefully enjoy said office..." This form, with Atwater's name inserted, is dated July 23, 1868, a year after the *Official Register* had him at the Seychelles.

Lincoln's Secretary of State was William H. Seward. His son, F. W. Seward, was assistant secretary of state on July 9, 1868 when Clarence Barton wrote to him on Atwater's behalf, calling attention "...to the request of the Connecticut Delegation and numerous other friends of Dorence Atwater for a consulship for him." She noted that Connecticut Governor James E. English had met with President Johnson and presented him with a petition signed by twenty senators and congressman, asking such a consulship for Dorence. The Connecticut supporters were hoping for Piraeus (the port of Athens) but that the Seychelles "would be more than acceptable." At the top of this very formal letter, someone has scribbled in pencil, "Reply that he was nominated for Seychelles on the _____ inst."

The file of Atwater supporters includes a previous Clara Barton letter with an illegible date, a letter dated June 16, 1868 from Congressman Hale, urging a consulship at Piraeus, and a June 8, 1868 petition signed by twenty-seven members of congress also requesting the Greek assignment. Did Dorence go to Piraeus? No. He went to Seychelles, as we have noted. But when? Probably in 1868. How did he get there? We don't know. What are the Seychelles?

They are a widely-scattered sprinkle of islands, some flat coral atolls, some mountainous and granitic peaks, in an 800-mile arc north of Madagascar and east of Kenya. The total area of all the islands is about twice that of Washington, D.C. (They are home to the most endangered animal species, the Seychelles sheath-tailed bat.) The principal island and site of the capital is Mahé, where Atwater took up his new duties.

The islands, uninhabited until French settlement in 1794, passed into British control in 1814; they ran affairs until independence in 1976. Unlike Connecticut with its icy winters, or Georgia with its blazing summers, the Seychelles stay within a few ticks of 80 degrees Fahrenheit and enjoy trade winds seven months of the year. But even a tropical paradise can have problems. On June 10, 1869, Joseph Lewis of New York City and P. Duvall of New Orleans sent an angry letter to the Secretary of State, written from Mahé.

We, the undersigned citizens of the United States, residing at Seychelles, beg to bring to your notice the very inefficient and careless manner in which Mr. Consul Atwater performs the duties of U.S. representative at this port. One of the subscribers, P. Duvall of Louisiana, arrived here from Madagascar a few months ago and for simply entering a boat belonging to the vessel, at the captain's order, to go onshore, although they did not land, he was fined [by the British authorities] $50 or three months' imprisonment. The manifest injustice of this sentence induced him to apply to the consul for advice and assistance but it was a useless proceeding. Mr. Atwater has evidently adopted a code of his own, so far as extending protection to American citizens is concerned. He would not interest himself in the matter. Duvall applied to Colonel Pike, U.S. consul at Mauritius — that gentleman took the affair in hand at once and the result is that his Excellency, the governor of Mauritius and Seychelles (affairs being administered here by a civil commissioner) has instructed the authorities to remit the fine. The other subscriber, Lewis, brought an action in the courts here against a resident and two witnesses belonging to an American vessel then in port who were properly summoned to appear. The vessel sailed two days before the day set for the trial and the case, on account on the absence of the two witnesses, fell to the ground. Believing it to be the duty of the consul to be sure all port regulations have been complied with by the shipmaster before delivering to him the vessel's papers, which according to law, the captain is obliged to deposit at the consulate and knowing in this instance that the ship had not been cleared at customs, Lewis applied to Mr. Atwater to ascertain how and by what means the vessel had been enabled to depart. Mr. Atwater refused to give any explanation, the only information gained by Lewis was the astonishing (to him) fact that the U.S. consulate at Seychelles is held "al fresco" at all events the interview took place in the yard of the consulate! We had supposed it to be the duty of a U.S. consul to countenance and protect law-abiding American citizens in all cases in which they may have been injured or oppressed, but to refuse them support when they have been guilty of any infraction of the laws, but Mr. Atwater seems to stand in terror of offending the English authorities here and clearly thinks he was sent here to uphold English interests and English honor, else what could have induced him to hoist a British union jack over the U.S. flag on the anniversary of Queen Victoria's birth, 24th of May, last? Was it to let the people here suppose that the U.S. are inferior to Great Britain? Or was it a deliberate insult to his country? The number of Americans here does not reach the teens but quite as much indignation has been expressed at this imbecile as if we numbered thousands. Dignity and intelligence are usually associated with a position of such importance as Mr. Dorence Atwater now holds but we are fain to know that as yet he has developed neither of those very necessary faculties. We have resided here a number of years and our opinion may not be unacceptable: Since 1858 the yearly average arrival of American vessels here is four, an interval of five or six months frequently intervenes. So it will be seen that there is very little for a consul to do — now, would not a consular agent under the control of the consul at Mauritius, of which Seychelles is only a dependency or district, be all that is requisite? We respectfully submit that, as the United States are represented at Mauritius by a consul (at which place 50-fold more official business is required of a consular officer than is required here) and as reports are rife here that Mr. Atwater receives 2,000 per annum for services he assuredly does not perform, a clerk, who has served in a consul's office, or some practical and experienced person be appointed, who, at least, is possessed of sufficient knowledge and courtesy and the usages of civilized nations not to fly an English flag over the stars and stripes from the consular flagstaff. Trusting our communication will receive the attention it deserves, we subscribe ourselves your obedient servants.

The letter from Messieurs Duvall and Lewis was dated June 10, 1869. Scribbled in the margin and dated November 1869 are the words "charges preferred." This usually means that formal charges against Atwater were instituted. What became of them?

The author has not been able to find documents to answer this question but it would appear that there may have been previous discontent with Atwater's services. On April 30, 1869, William A. Buckingham, governor of Connecticut, had written to Secretary of State Hamilton Fish, reminding Fish of Atwater's Andersonville service and concluding, "As the [consular] position may be too unimportant to attract the attention of many who desire foreign appointments, and as he has rendered services peculiarly valuable, I cherish the hope that he may not be removed." This certainly hints that someone had suggested removing him.

On May 12, 1869, Edward W. Whitaker, formerly an officer in Atwater's Connecticut squadron, and now, a passionate defender of veteran's rights, and an active member of several veterans organizations, wrote from his office in Washington D.C. to the

Secretary of State. "I beg you in the name of his thousands of friends in Connecticut to retain him in his [consular] appointment. He was a true and faithful soldier in my command during the war and I will vouch for his faithfulness to the present administration." (This last phrase illustrates the importance of political loyalty during the spoils system.)

In 1870, Atwater's job still seemed in peril. On April 4, Clara Barton wrote from Switzerland, "In a recent number of the New York Herald, I observe a list of the changes of consulates proposed by the bill under consideration by the present congress and regret to find that of my protégé, Dorence Atwater, among the number to be discontinued...for [his] good service, I asked this little consulate of 'Seychelles' for him...it's genial climate gradually restoring the strength and health he had lost in war and prison." She concluded that if the Seychelles position was abolished that he "be not entirely thrown out, but removed to some other post."

On May 21, 1870, the governor of Connecticut, William A. Buckingham, wrote to the Secretary of State, noting the closure of the Seychelles consulate and asking that Atwater be transferred to the newly opened consulate at Inagua, the most southerly island of the Bahamas. The internal decisions of the State Department remain obscure, but the 1871 *Official Register* lists, "Dorence Atwater, consul, Society Islands, Tahiti." Yet another and very different chapter of Dorence's life now opened. He was age twenty-six.

CHAPTER 8

Trouble in Paradise

Dorence Atwater was headed for Tahiti. Even today, there is much confusion in American minds about Tahiti, a mental mixture of long out-of-date sailors' yarns, wishful thinking, utopian dreams, and the exotic photographs in tourist brochures. At a resort on Moorea, I witnessed a bachelor fireman from Los Angeles who was hoping to fulfill his dreams of a carnal paradise. He'd been sitting poolside, drinking all afternoon, and attempting to pull the cocktail waitresses onto his lap. They were, indeed, Polynesian lovelies, with flowers in their long, dark hair, wearing brightly-colored pareos, and like most servers, flashing brilliant smiles — all part of the job. After a particularly vigorous attempt to capture one young woman, she slid away from him, giggling and smiling and remarked to a nearby colleague, "Il est le roi des cons." She assumed, correctly, that he spoke no French. Her remark, gently translated, meant, "He is king of the buttholes." Had he spent part of the morning walking down the nearby road, he would have passed a variety of churches, temples, and chapels. Christianity, in its manifold manifestations, runs deep in today's Polynesia. Tahiti today is not at all what he had thought. Like any place, it has a history and a culture, in fact, a very complex history and culture, all of which is relevant to our Andersonville survivor.

Most Americans speak no second language. We were witnesses to an "authentic" Tahitian feast being prepared on the beach. During the afternoon, the native staff had dug a great hole in the sand and built a roaring fire, heating a bed of volcanic rocks. Chickens, suckling pig, and vegetables were wrapped in wet leaves, placed on the coals, and covered with sand. Supper would be excavated hours later, fully cooked. The spectators to this pit-digging and fire-building included one of the local inhabitants, who remarked to a friend, "S'ils savait que ça devrait être du chien!" Roughly,

"They don't know that we usually cook a dog." (He assumed, incorrectly, that my wife was not fluent in French.) Even today, there is much room for cultural and linguistic misunderstanding. Imagine Dorence Atwater 120 years ago, a New England Yankee, speaking neither French nor Tahitian, arriving south of the equator to represent his nation.

Somewhere around 500 A.D. Polynesians from Tonga and Samoa settled on the island. The earliest western visitors, such as English sea captain Samuel Wallis in 1767, and the French explorer, Louis-Antoine Bouganville the following year, brought home wild and romantic tales of a happy, carefree, and partially naked paradise, with unlimited sexual availability and an abundance of delicious and unfamiliar foods, all in a salubrious climate, free from the annoying frosts, snow, and heavy clothing of northern Europe.

The visitors brought not only their curiosity and their lust, they also brought syphilis, typhus, smallpox, influenza, and alcoholism. The original population of around 50,000 dropped to a nadir of around 6,000.

The next phase of western influence grew out of the race of the European nations to become colonial powers. Portugal had Brazil and Angola. France had Canada and Algeria. Spain had México and half of South America. The Dutch had what is now Indonesia. The British had the east coast of North America and were moving into India. All of them were reaching for any corner of the world not yet taken. The two principal competitors for Tahiti were the French, aided by Catholic priests and the British, aided by Protestant missionaries. The first Mormon missionaries arrived in 1845 but tended to avoid the political arena.

The Polynesians were not living up to Jean Jacques Rousseau's idea of a peaceable kingdom. Tahiti and its nearby islands, like the Hawaiian Islands, were in a constant state of tribal warfare, mostly conducted with heavy clubs, with which they smashed in each other's skulls. The ancient controlling royalty of Tahiti had been the Teva lineage, powerful in themselves and allied with the old gods. Captain Cook threw his support — and muskets — behind a young chief named Tu, who was in conflict with several other tribes. Tu emerged dominant. For political and genealogical reasons, Tu changed his name to Tina and then to Mate. With his final victory, around 1790, he became Pomare I and founder of the Pomare Dynasty. On his death in 1803, his son took the throne as Pomare II and five years later, was forced to flee to Moorea after a military defeat. His fortunes improved in 1815 and he returned to rule Tahiti again. The missionaries had been educating his son, Prince Pomare III, to be the future king, while ignoring the young man's sister Aimata. Pomare II died in 1821, possibly of alcoholism, and the young Pomare III followed him to the grave only six years later. The overlooked sister, to everyone's surprise, not only became Pomare IV (also known as Pomare Vahine and Queen Pomare) but ruled for fifty years. These were not always peaceful years. She was driven into exile at least twice, including an 1843 sojourn on Raitea. She passed to her reward just a few years before Dorence Atwater arrived, and his long sojourn in Tahiti overlapped with the reign of Pomare Vahine's son, Pomare V, who signed over his kingdom to the French in 1880.

Like in America's Old West, opportunists, often men with shady pasts, drift into any area where turmoil and change have stirred the water. William Stewart was one such man. He had been a warrant officer in the British army in India, but soon arrived in Portugal without his uniform and took a Portuguese bride. Leaving her at home, he became a whisky smuggler in Australia until suddenly forced to flee that country. He was next heard of in Melanesia, trading in slaves and guns. It may have been the illegality of this work that sent him back to Portugal, where he persuaded his brother-in-law to put up $200,000 to invest in plantations in Tahiti.

In the summer of 1862, Stewart with six companions — all Irish Catholics — sailed into Papeete harbor and soon presented their credentials to the governor, Capt. Gaultier de la Richerie, who had been ordered to welcome investors. After a brief search, Stewart settled upon the huge valley of Atimaono as the place for his investment.

The island of Tahiti is shaped like a figure eight, two huge volcanic cones joined by a narrow isthmus. The largest land mass, Tahiti Nui, has the city of Papeete and much of the wealth. The smaller portion, Tahiti Iti, plays little part in our story. The most prosperous and powerful district ("commune" in French) is Papara, a huge wedge of land running south from the central mountains and ending in the broad swath of beaches, headlands, and harbors on Tahiti Nui's south coast. The District of Mataiea (also called Otutara) lies just to the east of Papara. Stewart had his eye on the 4,000 acres of Atimaono, adjacent to Papara. So did the 200 family groups who lived in Mataiea and claimed ancient and hereditary ownership of these 200 family parcels. Within each family group, a dozen or more individual families laid claim to sub parcels. All these groups were joined in a complex web of genealogies.

Like Alexander and the Gordian Knot, Stewart, aided by the governor and unknowable amounts of bribery, soon had clear title to the entire valley, dispossessing dozens of families who had lived on that land for close to a thousand years. His soon-to-be neighbors on adjacent Papara objected to this land grab by an obvious competitor. Each district had its own aristocracy and royalty, tied in various ways to the overall "kingship" of the Pomare dynasty — and to the future of Dorence Atwater.

The island of Huahine lies 75 miles northwest of Tahiti and in 1863 was ruled over by Queen Ariipaea Vahine. A brief digression into Tahitian terms shows the frequent use of "arii" in names. Arii meant royalty and/or aristocracy. The same word is seen in the Hawaiian language as "alii." A second important word is "vahine," which always designates female gender, and depending on the context, can mean woman, queen, consort, girlfriend, or mistress.

As Stewart settled into the work of converting his 4,000 ill-gotten acres into a working agricultural venture, he rented 300 acres from Teriifaatau, a niece of Queen Ariipaea. This niece was soon more than a landlord and, most probably, was for a time Stewart's vahine.

A plantation needs labor. There was no tradition of sustained wage labor in Tahiti, and Stewart's local employees would collect their wages and go home to play. Stewart soon hit upon a plan to import impoverished coolies from China. Each of them "signed" a contract. In return for working twelve hours a day, twenty-six days a month for seven years, each would receive room and board and at the end of the seven years, about $350. Total. By 1864, 1,200 Chinese had arrived and orange groves and cotton fields were soon flourishing, and bridges and roads were springing up, as well as Stewart's vast mansion, whose foundation stones were literally ripped from the ancient ceremonial platforms used to worship the Tahitian gods. Soirees and dances filled the halls with revelry. Now, what of his Papara neighbors?

Since Tahiti had no written language, the history of Papara is mainly by word of mouth and memorized genealogies, supplemented by the diaries of a few Christian missionaries, many of whom supported and armed the Pomare factions during a series of bloody wars and horrifying massacres. The major source for Papara's history is from the pen of the American journalist, Henry Brooks Adams, who recorded and published the recollections of Marau Taaroa, widow of Pomare V and last queen of Tahiti. She knew Dorence Atwater, and their lives had many intersections.

The recorded history of Papara begins to emerge from the memorized oral genealogies with the advent of the first Tati (1773 – 1854) whose many other names included Taura Atua i Patea. His relations with Pomare I were cordial, but on the first king's death in 1803 all that changed. Pomare II, also called Otoo, had no interest in sharing power and, aligned with Christian missionaries, armed Christian converts, and a small number of murderous European mercenaries, attacked Tati and his territory of Papara. Otoo's forces murdered women and children and any men they could capture. Tati fled first to the high mountains and then to Bora Bora, where he spent the years 1808 to 1812 in exile. In his absence, Opuhara became chief of Papara and on several occasions, defeated Pomare's forces. All that changed in 1815 at the battle of Fei-pi where a Christian musket ball ended Opuhara's life. Tati resumed the Papara chiefdom and reigned in relative peace until his death in 1854.

Leaping ahead a generation, we find his granddaughter Ari'itaimai, in 1842, marrying Alexander Salmon, bringing us another step closer to Dorence Atwater's long involvement in Tahiti. In general, Tahitian royalty were forbidden to marry non-Tahitians. What was special about Salmon? Why did he merit such a dispensation?

Salmon came from a family of Jewish bankers situated in London. Risky speculation and financial collapse prompted his departure from London and in 1839 he was in California, ten years too early for the Gold Rush. Finding few prospects in what was then a sleepy Mexican outpost, he set sail for Honolulu and Sydney, finally arriving in Tahiti in 1841. In what must be a tribute to his energy and adaptability, only a year later he was marrying into a royal family, with Ari'itaimai as his bride.

Salmon quickly adjusted to the swirling currents of Tahitian politics. (He must also have mastered the French and Tahitian languages.) The Catholic missionaries and their converts petitioned the government in Paris to make Tahiti a French protectorate. The protestant missionaries and their converts just as eagerly petitioned London, asking to become a British protectorate. Queen Pomare, caught in these conflicts, had been exiled to Raitea, 150 miles west of Tahiti. Salmon, with his wife, sailed to Raitea several times and was instrumental in obtaining her return and her acceptance of the new status of Tahiti.

The French had declared Tahiti a protectorate in 1842. The next year, a French admiral, acting on his own, declared that Tahiti had been "annexed." In 1844, the Queen fled to Raitea as a protestant missionary led an armed revolt against French rule. She returned when the French protectorate was reestablished. Salmon had fished in troubled waters and earned his credentials as a man of influence.

However, his principal interest lay in agriculture and in increasing the value of his wife's extensive holdings. At Papara, he planted the first moka coffee trees and established huge orange groves. His piggeries were very productive; he imported enormous cast iron kettles, with iron feet, for producing cooked pork. The excellent pasturage of Papara grew enormous cattle. After 1849, the California market for fruit and meat generated huge profits. In 1866, he had reached the pinnacle of his career. He was not only wealthy and married into royalty, he was president of the commercial court and member of the Colonial Council, and held the American consulship. At that moment of triumph, epidemic dysentery cut short his life. He left a fortune and nine children. His son, Tati (1850 –1918) became chief of Papara and a friend of Robert Louis Stevenson, Henry Adams, and Prince Oscar of Sweden. His son Alexander carried on the plantation at Papara. His daughter, Joanna Marauta'aroa Tepa' o Salmon married Pomare V and became the last queen of Tahiti. His daughter, Titaua married John Brander, who owned the first commercial house in Papeete.

This brings us to the relevant daughter, Arii'ino'ore Moetia Tepau Salmon (1848 – 1935). As Dorence Atwater wasted away in the Andersonville prison, he most certainly did not anticipate taking a South Seas princess as his bride, nor of having as his sister-in-law the queen of Tahiti.

CHAPTER 9

Rainbows and Storm Clouds

In 1868, Ulysses S. Grant, the architect of Union victory, was elected president. In 1871, he appointed Dorence as U.S. consul in Tahiti, replacing Francis Perkins. The *Alta California*, that state's leading newspaper, mentioned Dorence on the front page.

> San Francisco September 15, 1871. Consul to Tahiti— Mr. Dorence Atwater, recently appointed United States consul to Tahiti, is at present in the city, and will leave on Sunday on the *Greyhound*. Mr. Atwater was a sergeant in the Army of the Potomac in the late war. He did gallant service, and was taken prisoner at Gettysburg. For twenty-two months he was detained in southern prisons, eleven months of which he was confined in Andersonville Prison. When first captured he weighed a hundred and eighty pounds and when he was released he was a skeleton of ninety-five pounds. He furnished the government with a record of Union prisoners confined at that period. His appointment by President Grant is but a just recognition for the services rendered by him.

And the *Greyhound?* In that decade there were seventeen ships in United States Registry named Greyhound or Grayhound. The most likely candidate for Dorence's voyage was a 149-ton schooner built of yellow fir in San Francisco in 1869, registry number 85,036. She was owned and skippered by a Mr. Burns. Today, sailing to Tahiti in a schooner, a voyage of some six thousand miles, would be considered high adventure. In 1871, it was strictly business. As we shall see, Dorence Atwater would be no stranger to these waters.

His first claim to fame in his new job involved the notorious Captain Richard Veeder, skipper of the whaling ship *William Gifford*, out of New Bedford, Massachusetts. In those days, a whaler might be out of touch with her home port for years. The owners reposed their trust and their investment in the captain; at sea the captain's word was law. The literature is full of tyrannical and sadistic captains, most of whom did the job they were hired to do. The system did not work as well when the captain was a madman.

In 1871 as soon as Veeder rounded the tip of South America and burst out of the Straits of Magellan into the deep blue of the Pacific Ocean, he became unhinged. Whatever stores he had ordered for his ship, the list seems to have included vast quantities of rum. His first ports of call were in the Marquesas, most likely including Nukuhiva. This island group, six hundred miles northeast of Tahiti, had a population of 90,000 when "discovered" by whites. By the time of Veeder's visit the population was closer to 9,000, ruined by rum, syphilis, tuberculosis, small pox, and violent conflicts with the French army. Veeder was quick to hasten the decline of Marquesan culture. He took aboard a collection of local lovelies, and in between drunken bouts of carnal excess, stopped at many islands so that his new friends could go ashore and look for pretty seashells. Obviously, he was catching few whales for his employers.

It was customary for the lookout who first spotted a whale to receive extra pay. The clichéd, "Thar she blows," was not just a legend. In Veeder's case, he sent some of the women aloft and rewarded these consorts for spotting whales. But when they spotted a whale he rarely lowered the boats to pursue the valuable cetaceans. Instead, he returned to his bunk and resumed his horizontal activities. One of his sailors who had kept a diary noted that the captain had had women on board 210 days during that year. The crew did not challenge Veeder's absolute authority until May 1872, when the captain set a course directly for a reef, which would have killed all of them. After steering the ship away from danger, the crew saw their captain become further deranged. He beat his current favorite mistress and then came on deck with two loaded pistols, threatening murder. This was too much. The crew disarmed him, tied him up, and found their way to Tahiti, no easy task, since Veeder was the only man on board who knew how to navigate. At Papeete, Dorence took charge. He removed Veeder as skipper, hired a new and more sober skipper (who also knew how to navigate) and dispatched the ship to San Francisco to meet with the owner's agent. The owner, whose difficult signature seems to end in "Gifford," expressed his gratitude to Dorence in a letter sent from New Bedford, dated September 17, 1872.

Dorence Atwater, Esq., U.S. consul Tahiti. Dear Sir, I am just in receipt of your favor of July 3, 1872 enclosing draft for $12.65 being the balance of account as per receipt rendered for expenses incurred for transportation of the natives brought to Tahiti by Captain Veeder of the bark *William Gifford*. I have not before addressed you on the subject as I was so much astonished at the condition of Captain Veeder that it could not seem possible he could commit so flagrant a breach of trust and confidence as he has done, and sacrificed not only his own and the owners interest, but also the honor and feelings of his family. That a man of his age and former standing as a ship master in this community should stoop so low is truly astonishing. And to his wife and children it is worse than the announcement of his death. You are probably aware that my agent reached San Francisco, took possession of the *William Gifford*, recruited her for a voyage and home sailing from that port on the ninth of August. Permit me, sir, in closing to express for myself and co-owners, our hearty thanks and also the high esteem and regard we have for you for the promptness, energy, and economy you used in taking possession of our property and arresting what I am satisfied would eventually have been a wholesale sacrifice of ship and cargo, by doing which you have won the confidence of all who are acquainted with the details of this unpleasant affair, and hoping that if you ever visit this city you will feel free to call on me that I may more fully express to you the just appreciation we have of your management of this business.

In December 1874, Dorence's wartime superior, E. W. Whitaker, forwarded the letter to Secretary of State Hamilton Fish. "Please read the enclosed letter and observe the kind words of a New Bedford ship owner to young Dorence Atwater, the United States consul at Tahiti, who, by his promptness, energy, and faithfulness saved an American ship and cargo from the hands of a drunken captain. Please add the letter to those on file in your office in support of Atwater's promotion." Written on the margin of the ship owner's letter, in an unknown hand, is "5 May 1875 consulate. Tahiti. Dorence Atwater Recomd."

Consular duties did not seem to consume much of his time and Dorence cast about for ways to enrich himself. He was soon a partner in William Stewart's 4,000 acre enterprise in the Atimaono Valley. The 1,200 Chinese laborers had arrived in 1864. The following year the American Civil War ended. That war had pinched off much of the world's cotton supply and the long fiber Sea Island cotton of Atimaono was of the finest quality. But peace in the United States had opened the flood gates of competition and the prospect of vast riches from Stewart's plantation had begun to evaporate.

Stewart's in-laws back in Portugal, the Soarès family, were prudent folk. They had ordered him to put half the acres into coffee and sugar cane. Money was rolling in and a partnership with Stewart seemed like an excellent idea for Dorence. Out in the fields, the coolies were producing excellent crops; up on the hill Stewart's new mansion rang with laughter and music as the crème of Tahiti's society gathered for receptions, feasts, and gala balls. All seemed well; the party would last forever. But there was a worm in this shining apple — perhaps more than one worm. True, the money was rolling in, but it was barely enough to cover the enormous expenses of building the plantation. William Stewart's brother, James, always the family black sheep, had been up in the Tuamotus, trading on his brother's credit, without William's knowledge, and without making any money.

There were culture clashes. The two chief religious affiliations for the island had been French Catholic and British Protestant. Now there was a whole new cultural group: the Irish Catholic enclave of Stewart's Atimaono, with its Irish Catholic church and its Irish Catholic school, not to mention its huge numbers of "heathen Chinese." The Queen, Pomare Vahine, was strongly Protestant, as were her immediate followers, and she had grave doubts about this new center of power.

Even as Atwater joined forces with Stewart things were unraveling. In 1865 there had been a major riot on the plantation between two rival Chinese groups, fueled by some rum and the din of firecrackers. Many of the coolies were finishing their terms of service and returning to China. The ne'er-do-well brother, James Stewart, was caught "blackbirding," recruiting or enslaving black skinned Melanesians, for work on the plantation. One entire schooner load of these men had died of contagious disease before they picked a single cotton boll. Then James vanished, one step ahead of the law, and William's Australian bankers impounded his assets to pay for the bills that James had run up. Atwater was suspected of some wrong doing, but nothing was ever proved. By September 1873 William Stewart was legally bankrupt and died later that same month, vomiting blood, abandoned by all except one vahine, Tiare Gibson, who stayed with him to the end. The fields, the barns, the stables, the mansion — all lay empty and abandoned.

Atwater, who had survived worse crises, had kept his social ties open with Stewart's neighbors, the Salmons. The closeness of those ties was affirmed in a document in the files of the French administration. It commences "Etablissment Français de l'Océanie – le Tahiti – Acte de mariage entre Sieur Atwater, Dorence et Demoiselle Salmon, Ariinoore Moetia Tepau … le vingt sept du mois d'Octobre à dix heures de matin …" in translation, Dorence had married Moetia Salmon on October 27, 1875 at the Papeete City Hall, in a ceremony certified by Maximin Bonnet, registrar of vital statistics. He was thirty; she was twenty-seven. The documents note that the groom was unable to produce the death certificates of either his parents or his grandparents and that Dorence's and Moetia's intent to marry had been published on two previous Sundays. Both bride and groom affirmed that no marriage contract had been made. The witnesses were: James W. Dennet, captain, age fifty-four; Benjamin Franklin Chapman, merchant, age forty-four; Tati Salmon, planter, age twenty-two; and Temauiarii Maheanun (the handwriting is difficult) planter, age twenty-four.

Dorence's marriage to one of the wealthiest heiresses of Tahiti, just four years after his arrival, generated a certain degree of enmity. A San Francisco newspaper, alert to doings in the South Seas, used terms such as "an extraordinary marriage intrigue," and "beauty sacrificed to lust and ambition."

Were such comments the result of a narrow, almost incestuous, insular society, or were they the result of real character flaws? We do not know. We do know that a biographical directory quoted the French diplomat M. Gilbert-Pierre, who saw in Dorence "a blemished, flawed man… spurned by everyone here… and whose character is certainly not what one would expect in the consul of a great nation. He is, nevertheless, obsessed by the privileges attached to his position." Another biographer claimed that Dorence was seen by most as an honest, upright man, extremely skillful in managing his own affairs. Another writer called him a "phantom consul," doing consular business during short stays in Papeete. He spent a large part of his time at sea, visiting other islands or tending to business in San Francisco. Other writers say that the sea air was essential for his asthma.

In the 1800's a husband had much control over his wife's money. Some husbands destroyed the fortunes that they had married into. Well known American examples include the family of Virginia's favorite son, Robert E. Lee. His father, Lieut. Col. Henry Lee, known as "Light Horse Harry," married first to the "Divine Matilda," wasted her vast inheritance and then married the heiress Ann Carter, by whom he sired Robert E. Lee and Carter Lee. As Robert grew up he saw his mother reduced to poverty and his father fleeing the country one jump ahead of the sheriff. Carter spent the last of the family money on wine and women, while Robert's half brother, Henry, married and ruined another heiress, while siring a bastard upon his teenage sister-in-law. (Robert E. Lee was, of course, a shining exception to such Lee misbehavior.)

Did Dorence follow the pattern of the wayward Lees? Not at all. He strove mightily and successfully to improve the family fortunes opened to him by this marriage. By 1879 twenty-five acres of vanilla were springing up under the nourishing tropical sun of Papara. He was deeply involved in the mother-of-pearl trade in the Tuamotu archipelago. His fleet of schooners furrowed the ocean throughout Polynesia and along the long track to California. With his friend Robert Louis Stevenson, then the best known writer in America, Dorence founded a steamship line, the first to run between Tahiti and San Francisco. Stevenson's 1894 book *The Ebb Tide,* which described his friendship with Atwater, deplored the exploitation of the South Seas by the colonial powers.

In 1888, Dorence resigned as U.S. consul in Tahiti, but certainly continued to have many political opinions. Around 1900, he was associated with a rumor that Tahiti was to be sold to the United States for 200,000 gold francs. A few years later, Dorence was floating another rumor, as described in the August 3, 1906 New York *Times*.

BRITAIN MAY GET TAHITI. BELIEF THAT FRANCE WILL OBTAIN OTHER TERRITORY IN EXCHANGE. Special to the New York Times. San Francisco, August 2. It is reported from Tahiti that that island paradise as well as others of the Society Islands will soon be transferred by France to Great Britain. T. [sic] Atwater, one of the largest planters in Tahiti, and formerly American consul at Papeete, is authority for the statement. For sometime French stores, ammunition, and much vital machinery have been gradually withdrawn and military and naval forces have been recalled. The belief at Papeete is that the islands will be exchanged with Great Britain for other possessions. The natives themselves are mostly indifferent, but some of the leaders are openly pro-British, having English blood in their veins and having been educated in England. Mr. Atwater says there is not the least doubt of the transfer of Tahiti to Great Britain. Every French soldier has been recalled, the government buildings have been abandoned, and all the stores have been removed. The only government vessel left is the Little Zell. The islands, it is said, are not prosperous now, and everything is mortgaged. The islands were once the seat of a great copra trade but this has declined. They also have one of the largest pearl beds in the world. Lately, they have been visited by tourists every year.

It is worth noting the presence of "the government vessel... the Little Zell." That gun-boat will play a part in a later episode of the story of Dorence Atwater. Looking back for a moment down the road of Dorence's life, as he began his brief association with William Stewart, there were 1,200 Chinese laboring on the Atimaono Plantation. Did these men play a part in post-Stewart Tahiti? Mr. Jimmy Ly, associated with the Philanthropic Association at Papeete, wrote to the author, "I sincerely regret to inform you that there is unfortunately very little information about that period, even from the Chinese themselves. Most of the Chinese from the Atimaono Plantations... returned to the homeland, very few settled on the island. No written document has ever been preserved for that period... As for the present Chinese community itself, most of the original members came in from a later period, since 1900. Since there are not many dependable historical facts, I sincerely hope that the few items I have given to you will be of any help". Mr. Ly suggested *The Tahitian Chinese Community* by Richard Moench (Harvard University Press).

The late 1800's found Dorence Atwater married, corpulent, and rich. He owned schooners, steamships, and plantations. He was deeply enmeshed in Tahitian aristocratic society and, presumably, fluent in French and Tahitian. Back home, events were moving which would benefit him in non-financial ways.

DORENCE ATWATER.

Dorence Atwater late in life. In the 1800s, no one had ever heard of cholesterol, or triglycerides, or jogging, or anorexia, or six-pack abs. Being well-nourished meant wealth and prosperity. William Howard Taft was so fat he got stuck in the White House bathtub. Here, our protagonist wears a well-cut suit and seems fully recovered from the walking skeleton that emerged from the Confederate prison system.

His hometown was Terryville, Connecticut. Just a few miles away, in 1895, the town of Plymouth was celebrating its centennial. The numerous speeches and declamations were collected in a thick volume *Centennial Celebration of the Town of Plymouth*, reprinted in 1995 at the time of Plymouth's bicentennial. Judge Joseph Sheldon of New Haven addressed "a few words" to the 1895 crowd on the subject of Dorence Atwater. Twenty-two hundred words later, he concluded his summary of the life and service of Atwater, a story already told in these pages and then turned his attention to Adjutant-General Townsend, one of Atwater's chief persecutors.

Adjutant-General Townsend, I am informed, is now dead. His conduct in this case may possibly carry his name and fame further than all his honorable career in the Army. But it ought to be remembered that his persistent error in this case was not really what it seems on the surface. Even now at the distance of thirty years. It was not all together that a very bat-eyed, wrong-headed martinet was simply abusing power in the old, old way. It ought to be remembered that it was then a time of quick harsh judgments against subordinates, on the part of those in command, at the end of a long and irritating war - - that money-making schemes of every vile kind were being sprung upon the government on every side, and that his soldierly instincts revolted against them, every one. He seems to have mistaken Atwater for one of these money-making harpies. He cherished, perhaps, a habitual high sense of the honor and the duty of a soldier. Atwater had been disrespectful to the adjutant-general's office in a matter in which not only his honor was involved, but also the bleeding hearts of thousands of his countrymen were involved, for whom he had braved death in its most terrible form at the hands of the Confederates. The adjutant-general would have been incapable of acting the strange part he did act in this case if he had really seen the whole case, and his own part in it with any moral perspective. If he had realized that he was acting a dreadful part in one of the saddest tragedies of the war. Whether he lived to regret it, I do not know. It is quite probable that he did, for he often afterwards kindly inquired about Atwater after powerful friends had gathered around him, and the Chairman of the Committee on Military Affairs of the Senate, Henry Wilson of Massachusetts had become his friend and benefactor and Atwater was widely recognized as one of the modest, true heroes of the war. It is a pity, I think, that in this life they had not met and passed an act of formal forgiveness and amnesty for a cruel wrong. Jefferson Davis himself, and all but Wirtz, among the Confederates, have long since been forgiven. Their great violations of all law, human and divine, have been wisely passed over.

Judge Sheldon concluded that since amnesty had been extended to all the leaders of the Confederacy that we should do the same for Townsend. "I… recommend him to the mercy of that great court-martial of history, from which, for a soldier, there is no appeal." The judge then proposed a resolution asking its congressional delegation to introduce legislation pardoning Atwater, a resolution adopted by those attending the centennial celebration. Three years later, Congress issued Atwater's pardon.

The next speaker was Clara Barton, "Classed… as the greatest heroine America has ever produced." Miss Barton was then seventy-four years old. She reminded her audience that for thirty years she had asked for justice for Atwater and that for thirty years she had kept in a special cabinet a copy of his dishonorable discharge, together with battered cups and spoons and ladles, picked off the abandoned acres of Andersonville's stockade.

I have waited and waited, lo, these thirty years for the state of Connecticut to ask the government to draw that [document] out of my hands. I would have replaced it by an honorable discharge such as it deserves. It waits; it is there, and it lies side by side with the relics of that fated prison. I only ask: shall I keep it? Men of Connecticut, men of Plymouth, shall I keep it there, or will you direct the government to demand it of me? I will surrender it [the dishonorable discharge certificate] when you do." (At the end of her address three cheers were given for Miss Barton.)

Even at this point in his life Atwater could be at the center of a storm. He was not only rich and honored, but the stain of the dishonorable discharge had been lifted from his shoulders. In the town of Terryville is Baldwin Park and the trustees of that park, led by Judge Jason Fenn, thought it time to honor Dorence with a memorial. The custom of the time was to install a surplus cannon along with a suitably inscribed tablet. A Rodman cannon, no longer used, was available from a fort at Boston Harbor and the War Department approved its donation. The Rodman gun was not only authentic, it was so heavy that in over a century in Baldwin Park, no one has stolen it. (The smallest caliber Rodman weighed over 8,000 pounds.)

Here the memorial cannon faces out over a peaceful neighborhood. The little pond no longer exists. Rodman invented a method of iron casting which was a remarkable technological advance, and marked the pinnacle of muzzle-loading weapons.

The cost of transporting the cannon to Terryville was $175 ($1,300 in today's money), paid for by Judge Fenn. The granite stand, inscribed tablet, and installation would be another four hundred dollars. Just as construction was about to begin there was a protest. Someone's nose was out of joint. In this case it was the Gilbert W. Thompson post of the Grand Army of the Republic, located in nearby Bristol. What Thompson himself, who had served in the 16th Connecticut Infantry, would have thought of this mean-spirited vendetta is, of course, unknowable. But those acting in his name protested loudly that Atwater had received a dishonorable discharge and had served prison time for stealing a government document. Those familiar with earlier pages of this book will see that they may have oversimplified the story. At the height of the Bristol-Terryville conflict Dorence's brother, Richard Atwater, invited the Bristol veterans to Terryville, to debate the matter face to face. That was the end of the protest.

The plaque and cannon mounting was soon completed and were officially dedicated on Memorial Day 1907, with Clara Barton in attendance. In 1908, Dorence Atwater and his Tahitian wife paid a visit to Terryville and viewed the memorial. Crowds gathered to see the now legendary figure and his equally legendary Polynesian spouse. Then the two boarded a train, crossed the continent to San Francisco, caught a ship to Tahiti and returned to their island home. He would not see his birthplace again.

CHAPTER 10

Moetia Becomes a Widow

It seems likely that Dorence regarded his 1908 visit to Terryville as a step in settling his earthly affairs, an adding up of the columns of his moral and personal accounting, a closing of the circle of life. He had been weakened by years of sickness, perhaps malaria caught during his time in the American south, and certainly not cured in the warm and humid air of Tahiti.

On September 20, 1910, he came under the care of Dr. James W. Ward, who kept offices at 391 Sutter Street in San Francisco. Dorence and Moetia stayed at the Hotel Normandie (corner of Sutter and Gough Streets) and saw Dr. Ward frequently. The old soldier's health took a turn for the worse on November 28, 1910 and at 10:30 that night his heart stopped forever. The death certificate gives the cause as "Aneurism aorta with contributory acute bronchitis."

Dorence wished to be buried in Tahiti. His body was taken to the undertaking and embalming establishment of Samuel McFadden at 1070 Haight Street. A long and accurate obituary in the November 30, 1910 San Francisco *Chronicle*, entitled — "Civil War Veteran is Called by Death" — contained one minor error, more of an over simplification. "The Government, being informed of his records, demanded a copy of them. This Atwater refused unless he was compensated and he was there upon tried by court-martial and dishonorably dismissed from the Army." We also learned from the *Chronicle* that Dorence had spent most of 1895 - 1910 in San Francisco. On the death certificate, Moetia stated that he had lived in California for the previous five years. The New York *Times* on November 30, 1910, also ran an obituary — "Dorence Atwater Dead" — based on information from Dorence's brother Francis, "A newspaper publisher of Meriden, Connecticut."

Two months later, apparently thoroughly embalmed, he set off on his final sea voyage. On January 10, 1911, an elaborate cortege, including fifty veterans from the Lincoln Post, Grand Army of the Republic, saw him off at the pier. Twelve days later his ship tied up at Papeete's harbor. Traditional pallbearers, most in evidence at royal funerals, gently slid the huge casket down a ramp from the ship's deck onto a wagon, and escorted the body for the twenty-two mile trip to Papara. Dorence Atwater was home.

Dorence Atwater's huge casket, bedecked with flowers, has arrived at Papeete and is being eased down a ramp onto a waiting wagon. The men in the ceremonial white coats are part of an honor guard from Papara.

In 1921, Frederick O'Brien published an account of his several months in Papara. He described the village, with its Chinese stores, a Catholic church, and the Protestant church, where Dorence was buried. O'Brien recorded the inscription on the stele above his tomb.

In memory of Dorence Atwater, beloved husband of Ariiinoore Moetia Salmon. Born at Terryville, Connecticut, February 3, 1845. Died at San Francisco, California, November 28, 1910. As a last tribute to his name there was erected in his native state a monument with this inscription: "This memorial is dedicated to our fellow-townsman, Dorence Atwater, for his patriotism in preserving to this nation the names of 13,000 soldiers who died while prisoners at Andersonville, Georgia. He builded better than he knew; some day per chance, in surprise, he may awake to learn: He builded a monument more enduring than brass." Tupuataaroa.

"Tupuataaroa" means wise man in Tahitian. O'Brien noted the widow's melancholy. "She mourned her dead." Tati, who was O'Brien's host on this trip through Papara, described the great feast when the church was dedicated. The crowd of three thousand consumed two hundred and fifty pigs, fifteen hundred chickens, and fish too numerous to count.

The other side of the polished granite stele has this engraving:

Dorence Atwater at the age of 16, entered the Union Army as a volunteer with Kilpatrick's Cavalry in the war of 1861 – 1865. He was captured by Confederate Scouts disguised as Union Soldiers in July 1863, while carrying dispatches, and was taken to Belle Island Prison where he remained five months. From here he was taken to Smith's Tobacco Factory Prison and in February 1864 sent to Andersonville Prison with four hundred other prisoners where he was kept inside the stockade until May and then sent to the hospital. On June 15th, he was paroled and detailed to Surgeon J.A. White's office to keep the daily record of deaths of Federal prisoners. Suspecting the Rebel Government was withholding the facts of the daily mortality from the Federal Government, he began in the latter part of August 1864 to secretly copy the entire lists of dead prisoners in which he succeeded at the risk of his life and brought them safely through the lines in March 1865. To these lists is due the fact that the 13,000 Union Soldiers buried at Andersonville were identified, allowing the surviving relatives of the martyred dead to learn the fate of their loved ones. On July 1867 the state of Connecticut presented him a memorial worded as follows: "In grateful remembrance of the courage and patriotism by him displayed in the late war for the suppression of the rebellion and preservation of constitutional liberty." He was appointed consul of Seychelles Islands July 23, 1868 and transferred to Tahiti July 28, 1871, but in 1888 due to ill health he resigned this service to his country.

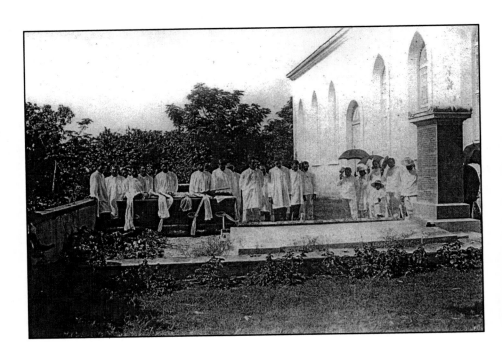

At the Protestant church in Papara, men wearing the coats that honor the dead of high rank, prepare to lower the casket into its tomb. At the right is the engraved granite stele.

The commemorative stele, engraved on both sides, tells of Atwater's life and accomplishments. The Protestant church is located at PK (Post kilometer) 36, on the main road through Papara.

(As of July 2008, Pastor Adrien Flores, of "le Temple Protestant de Papara," assured Rev. A. H. Ledoux by telephone that Atwater's monument is next to the church at PK 36, fully visible to any visitor. For those wishing to check on the future status of Atwater's monument, the phone number 689-574-110. Speak in French. If the number has changed, Google <L'annuaire official de Polynésie Française – Pages Jaunes.> In the search page query box, type Protestant. Scroll through the churches until you find Papara.)

Moetia was faced with many decisions. She had brought the inherited wealth into the marriage many years ago, but Dorence was the business man. She faced an uncertain future without his fiscal guidance. Among the tasks ahead was investigating the benefits that might be due her as the widow of a Civil War veteran. This would prove more exasperating than she could have anticipated. It would involve correspondence that had to make an 18,000 mile roundtrip, with intermediate stops for translation from French into English and back. That correspondence and the story of its ins and outs would also involve the saga of "Little Zell."

CHAPTER 11

Worse Than Pulling Teeth.

The fabric of Dorence and Moetia's life together was woven of many threads, each seemingly disparate, yet each eventually joining to form the complete tapestry of those years, with all its lights and shadows.

One thread is a present day occurrence. The scuba boat has come to rest in thirty meters of water off the Motu Uta breakwater of Papeete harbor. Each diver takes a first breath on his regulator to check the air flow, then tumbles backwards into the water. Minutes later their destination emerges from the blue mist of the sea: a curved hull, a few vertical pieces of coral-encrusted steel. It is the wreck of *La Zélée*, literally "The Zealous One," a French gunboat.

Now it is 1893 and Grover Cleveland has just been elected President. The rich and powerful of the nation are gathered for the Inaugural Ball in a huge brick building on F Street. Its enormously high atrium, made possible by some of the world's tallest Corinthian columns, easily holds the throng of cummerbunds, white ties, and elegant gowns. Outside in the starlight, a ceramic frieze wraps around the building, a parade of soldiers, sailors, cannons, horses, caissons, telling the structure's daytime function. Today it is the National Building Museum. In 1893 its sole purpose was to hold regiments of clerks, copyists, and pension examiners. It was the Pension Building.

In 1862, the Federal Government began issuing pensions to soldiers and sailors whose disabilities were "a direct consequence ... of military duty" or developed after combat "from ... diseases contracted while in military service." The dollar amount of the pension reflected the degree of disability and the previous military rank. Widows received an amount based on full disability. The

Grand Army of the Republic, a veteran's lobby group closely allied with the Republican Party, constantly pushed for increased benefits. In 1890, any disability, service connected or not, might qualify. By 1906 old age alone qualified a veteran for benefits. The October 5, 1893 New York *Times* pointed to the vast cost of the system, which was then more than the entire budget of the active Army, Navy, and Marine Corps. There were endless charges of fraud and corruption, especially related to very young women who married very old veterans, men with one foot in the grave, just one missed heartbeat from generating a widow's pension.

After the janitor had cleared away the debris from the Inaugural Ball, the clerks were back, hunched over their desks. By 1893, the emphasis had switched from issuing pensions to the truly wounded to ferreting out false and ineligible claimants.

Our scene changes again. It is now June 29, 1864, at Reams Station, Virginia. Captain Edward W. Whitaker, First Connecticut Cavalry, with an escort, breaks through an entire Confederate division to deliver dispatches to General Meade. Half of the escort is killed or wounded, but the dispatches go through. Whitaker received the Medal of Honor and in 1865 is brevetted brigadier general for "gallantry and uniform good conduct." In 1916 he is well settled into his new professions, patent attorney, and advocate for pension applicants and their widows.

In August 1914 the great powers of Europe were at each other's throats. The Germans, once again, invaded France and, once again, raped Belgium. The Italians and the Austro-Hungarians bloodied the snows of the Alps. Troops from Australia and India joined the British in France.

Mostly forgotten now, Germany held control of the Marianas, a widely scattered island group between New Guinea and Japan. The German Pacific fleet was led by two powerful coal-burning armored cruisers, the *Scharnhorst* and the *Gneisenau*, commanded by Admiral Maximilian von Spee. As soon as the telegraph brought word of events in Europe, von Spee set off to wreak havoc on British and French possessions in the Pacific — and to find coal. After a rendezvous at Christmas Island his fleet arrived at British Samoa on September 14th, but the telegraph had preceded him. The harbor was empty. September 21st found them at Bora Bora where, pretending to be French cruisers, they obtained supplies. The following day, lookouts at Papeete saw the western horizon blackened by coal smoke. Soon heavy German shells were tearing up Papeete and sinking "little Zell." The one worthwhile objective was the island's coal depot which the French had managed to set on fire. With nothing worth stealing, the Germans lobbed a few more shells into the now-burning town and headed for the Atlantic Ocean. An unusually sarcastic letter to the editor of the New York *Times* (October 7, 1914) by a Massachusetts Institute of Technology professor, gives one view of the proceedings.

Tahiti Island — Its Bombardment by Germany not a Valiant Exploit. Today's papers tell us of another splendid German victory. The town of Papeete, on the island of Tahiti is half destroyed by two German cruisers which bombarded it at the same time that they sank a small French gunboat. As your readers may not appreciate this heroic feat of German Arms, I write to explain that Papeete is a quiet South Sea island town of frame houses and native huts nestling among groves of palms and coconut trees on the shore of one of the most beautiful islands of the world. The harbor is open, but protected from the sea by a narrow barrier reef of coral, and there are no fortifications at all. From the open sea the whole town and bay are visible. What a great accomplishment! Two cruisers come to this happy island, destroy half a town, necessarily killing and wounding many, and sail away victorious to sea. Think of the satisfaction of the officers of those two German cruisers. With no possible benefit to Germany (since the French gunboat *Zélée* was small and dismantled) and without risk to themselves, they destroyed the homes, property, and lives of peaceful people. In degree it even surpasses the German exploits at Louvain and Rheims. If any of your readers are interested in the scenes of this German triumph they may be found in the National Geographic magazine for October 1911.

Some of the buildings destroyed in the bombardment were owned by Moetia Atwater. It is unlikely that they were insured against acts of war, so von Spee's attack cost her dearly. Admiral von Spee also had his losses. After an initial victory, in which he sank HMS *Good Hope* and HMS *Monmouth* off the coast of Chile, von Spee's fleet was destroyed in December 1914, killing him, his two sons, and 2,000 other men off the Falkland Islands.

This photograph shows the armored cruiser *Scharnhorst*, the flag ship of Rear Admiral Maximilian von Spee, commander of Germany's Cruiser Squadron in East Asia. The heavy clouds of black smoke reveal the weakness of his fleet: the constant need for coal, something scarce in a geologic region of coral reefs and igneous islands. With von Spee were the cruiser *Geneisenau* and the light cruisers *Emden* and *Nürnberg.*

The destruction of her Papeete property may have prompted her "Widows' Declaration for Pension" filed and notarized in San Francisco February 24, 1916. In it, she summarized Dorence's military service and described "malignant intermittent fever [probably malaria] which developed complications that resulted in his death." She cited their 1875 marriage and appointed Edward W. Whitaker of Washington D.C. as her attorney. Her residence: The Manx Hotel, San Francisco. This application was forwarded to G. M. Saltzgaber, Commissioner of Pensions, by Whitaker on February 29, 1916, with this handwritten note:

> Dear Sir: I herewith file an application for pension by the widow of one of my "boys of 1861" in the Second New York Cavalry. I am sure his prison life in Andersonville was the primary cause of his death. He belongs to a strong long-lived family. His torture in Andersonville and from a ring [as in criminal gang] in the War Department so destroyed his vitality that when I got a physician to examine him he fell in a faint as his chest was being examined. We induced the President to appoint him a consul at some islands in the Indian Ocean where his life was prolonged. While there he married this applicant. Copies of marriage and death records herewith enclosed. Please hasten settlement.

On April 4, 1916 the Pension Bureau received a three page certified, translated copy of her Tahitian marriage records, the same one

summarized earlier in this book. Two weeks later the Pension
Bureau rejected her claim "on the ground that soldier's death from
aneurism of the aorta not shown to have been due to his military
service, there being no record in the War Department, medical, or
other evidence connecting said death cause with soldier's service
in the line of duty, and you are manifestly unable to furnish such
evidence. You are further advised that as you married the soldier
prior to June 27, 1890, you may have title to pension under the act
of April 19, 1908, a blank form of application under said act being
herewith enclosed, which you are at liberty to fill out, execute, and
return to this bureau for consideration."

She replied to the rejection in a letter dated September 29, 1916. She
noted that the rejection letter had not reached her in Tahiti until
August 30, 1916, a travel time of five months. She acknowledged
that the immediate cause of death was the aortic aneurism, but
"during the twenty years of service as United States Consul ... he
suffered greatly from what the prison life in Andersonville had
done to him ... of the men that escaped from that hell of a prison —
none came out sound in body and health." On January 3, 1917
she filed a new application giving the same data. For nine months
the Pension Bureau made no reply. Whitaker's letter to Pension
Commissioner Saltzgaber, dated September 24, 1917 tells the story
of pension claim application number 1061830.

> 756 Rock Creek Church Road, Washington, D.C.
> September 24, 1917, marked "Personal." Dear
> Commissioner and Comrade. I much regret I cannot
> see you in person. I write to protest against the
> unnecessary delay in settling the pension claim of the
> widow of one of my cavalry comrades. The original
> claim should have been granted long ago, as I know
> his death due to his fifteen months imprisonment
> in Andersonville, but your over astute medical and
> legal clerks rejected it. Then a new claim was filed

under Act of April 19, 1908, and September 8, 1916, which has been unnecessarily held up and the settlement delayed by your Law Division quibbling over my recognition as attorney. As a proper power of attorney was filed to authorize me to prosecute the only claim pending, which I had duly filed, I have insisted on prompt recognition and then the early settlement of this very meritorious claim by a distressed widow residing in the distant Society Islands. If you knew, as I do, of the cruelty and torture that shortened the life of the brave soldier and the destruction of the widow's home in Tahiti by the Germans in the present war, you would order this claim made special and promptly settled. Confident that you will do something, I remain, as ever, your comrade E. W. Whitaker.

Now, two years have passed. Have the gears in the machinery of the Pension Bureau stopped? Was Dorence's widow the victim of lingering resentment regarding his defiance of the Adjutant-General back in the 1860's? In an attempt to move things along, on September 27, 1919 (nothing seems to have happened in 1918) Whitaker wrote to the Bureau, enclosing his personal affidavit, vouching for Dorence's excellent service in combat and adding a personal note. "[This claim] … has been long neglected by your office and I ask an early settlement. Thanking you in advance for your personal aid in your great and busy office."

Two weeks passed, two weeks with no reply. Whitaker wrote again, on October 5, 1919. "I earnestly solicit from you an order to your subordinates to immediately make the above named widow's claim special and grant it without more delay. She is in need of the [illegible] allowance and the delays in settlement of both of her claims have been as cruel and unnecessary as was the treatment of her soldier husband by that infamous ring in the War Department that induced him to ask his wife to take his body to her house for burial." (Apparently Atwater did not want to be buried in the United States, whose government had treated him so badly.)

This plea, a mixture of anger and desperation, had an effect. Only four days later, the Pension Commissioner wrote to the Chief of the Civil War Division: "It is believed from the evidence that a prima facie case has been made out and established, but it is not believed that ex parte evidence can be obtained to satisfactually settle case [a stellar example of bureaucratese, which used both the passive voice and unnecessary legal jargon] please have the case prepared and submitted through the Board of Review to the Special Examination Division for reference to the Special Examiner whose territory includes San Francisco, California, for the initial examination, and claimant's statement, and for the purpose of obtaining evidence as to the legal widowhood of the claimant." The Special Examiner, I.D. Laferty, scheduled five depositions for November 13, 1919 at his office in San Francisco. A stenographer rendered the statements onto typed sheets, which were signed by both the deponent and by the pension examiner. The first and longest deposition was that of the widow herself.

On this thirteenth day of November 1919 at San Francisco County of San Francisco, state of California before me, I.D. Laferty, a Special Examiner of the Bureau of Pensions personally appeared Ariiinoore Moetia Atwater who, being by me first duly sworn to answer truly all interrogatories propounded to her during this special examination of aforesaid claim for pension deposes and says: I am sixty-eight years of age: My postal address is Papeete, Tahiti, Society Islands. I have no occupation. I am at the present time stopping at the Plaza Hotel, this city, but day after tomorrow, Saturday the fifteenth I sail for home and do not expect to return under six months anyway. I have been here now six weeks or two months. My home however is in Papeete. My full and correct name is Ariiinoore Moetia Atwater and I am the person seeking pension as the widow of Dorence Atwater who died in this city November 1910. I took his body back to Papeete and buried it there. I never had any given name save Ariiinoore nor no middle name except Moetia. I am known by those who know me well as Moetia. My maiden name was Salmon, daughter of Alexander Salmon, an Englishman and my mother was a native woman. Both are dead. I have no brothers, but have one sister living in Papeete. I have no relatives at all in this country. I married Mr. Atwater in Papeete. We were married by the French officials (Tahiti is a French Colony) but I do not remember the date of the marriage but it must have been more than thirty-seven years ago. I do not remember my age at the time I married him. He was the American Consul there at the time I married him and I had known him about two years prior to our marriage. I came to know him because the consulate was just opposite our house. He was a very sick man and my mother would send nurses to care for him. I never had been married before I married Mr. Atwater. That was my first marriage. Marriages save by the duly constituted authorities were not and are not recognized. However, I never married or attempted to marry according to any local custom. I never gave birth to a child or children. We were never divorced but lived together as man and wife from the date of our marriage until he died. Occasionally he came to the states without me but we never parted in anger and there was never any separation at all. When he would make a trip to the states he did so for his health and frequently would come right back on the same boat. He was the consul there to within perhaps five years of his death, resigning on account of his health. We had our home there but came here and went to other places, he going in search of health, and but it was here that he finally took ill and died. He has two brothers living Richard Atwater, Hartford, Connecticut and Francis Atwater New Haven, Connecticut. Richard is, I am advised, employed in the state library while Francis is a newspaper man and has been a member of Congress. There are no sisters living as far as I know. Richard is older while Francis was or is younger than my late husband. My husband was never married before he married me so far as I know or ever heard or suspected. I am sure that I was his first wife. His brothers will know that I was his first and only wife. I have not remarried since the death of Mr. Atwater. I took his body back to Papeete a year after he died. While my home is in Papeete I have been in this city on several different occasions, first the year of the Exposition (1915) and two or three years since. There are folks here who know about my life, since the death of my husband, mainly Mrs. Turner, Mrs. Preston, Captain Turner and will know that I have not remarried, ceremonially or otherwise, since the death of my husband, will also know that we lived together as man and wife without divorce until he died. My attorney is a Mr. Cooper but I have none in this pension claim. I have not nor promised anyone a fee. I understand that I have the right to be present during the investigation of my claim if I so elect.

The other deponents covered much of the same ground, and I will summarize here only that which adds fresh information. Louis Turner, a sixty-three year old married surveyor, was a ship captain on the run to Tahiti while Dorence was consul. He recalled that Moetia and Dorence were married, that neither was married before, and that she has not remarried. He further recalled that they made many passages with him between Tahiti and San Francisco, and described her as having a good reputation. Marian

Turner, age fifty-eight, the wife of Louis, had known the claimant for at least thirty years. She knew them during many sea voyages and frequently saw Moetia in San Francisco. Charles H. Adams, age fifty-one, assistant secretary of the Merchant's Exchange, had known Moetia for sixteen years. She had been friends with Adams' parents. She often visited him when she was in San Francisco. "At one time she had [financial] means, [but] lost very heavily during the war." Cora Preston, widow, age forty-five lived at 1024 Leavenworth Street and had known the Atwaters for twenty-five years. "He died here in the Hotel Normandie. I was present at his burial. She has not remarried I am positive."

The following day, Laferty deposed one more witness, Emily Grant, the wife of an industrial engineer. "I was born on Samoa but lived in Tahiti from age six to age eighteen. I knew him as American Consul. I was chums with Moetia's younger sister. I know this was the claimant's only marriage. She has just returned from France and is on her way to Tahiti." That same day, November 14, 1919, Laferty wrote to the home office in Washington D.C. "She claims she has passage on a ship leaving tomorrow. Though claimant is a wealthy woman and has no special need of this pension, I concluded to take up her claim now, the above in explanation of my taking it up so much out of order. Claimant's reputation is good in all respects. She hobnobs with the better class of persons here, all of whom speak well of her." He concluded that she was indeed a widow who had never remarried, but he now had doubts about Atwater himself. [!] "I think it well to look a little into his career before he went to Tahiti as consul… I recommend further examination … as to non-prior marriage by soldier." He suggested taking depositions from Atwater's brothers.

(What could this Special Examiner have been thinking? That Dorence was married at age sixteen before he went in the army? That he had gotten married during the Battle of Gettysburg? Or during his stay in Andersonville? Or while sweating in Georgia marking graves? Or while in Albany Prison? He had a few months between prison and the Seychelles in which to seek a bride, but that seems unlikely. This search for a "non-prior marriage" certainly sounds like an obsessive bit of bureaucratic lunacy, rather than a careful safe-guarding of the American taxpayer's wallet, but the documents speak louder than the author's opinion.)

On December 3, 1919, in Connecticut, Francis Atwater testified, "There is absolutely no question that she is the legal widow of my brother Dorence Atwater." Two days later, Catherine Dikeman, a seventy year-old widow, told the deposer that her brother Dorence enlisted in the Army when he was sixteen. She was certain that this was the first and only marriage for both her brother and for Moetia.

Sometime in 1920, Moetia's application was finally approved. The whole process had taken four years, even with the active intercession of her attorney, Brevet Brig. Gen. Whitaker.

Fifteen years later, Scudder Mersman, U.S. Vice Consul at Tahiti, reported to the State Department of the death of Ariii Moetia Atwater. She was eighty-seven. His report has a few details. She died at 11 p.m. on August 13, 1935 from a fractured femur followed by bed sores. She died at the home of Princess Terii nui o Tahiti Pomare in Papeete and was buried in the family tomb at the French Protestant Church in Papara. Her husband had been Consul at Tahiti from October 26, 1871 to March 14, 1888. "She was the sister of Madame Marau Salmon, ex Queen of Tahiti, who died recently. Mrs. Atwater left no estate of any value, having deeded her considerable properties to her sister and nieces several years ago in return for a life income." At the time of her death she had been receiving a United States pension of forty dollars a month.

CHAPTER 12

Recessional

One of the delusions of current society is the notion of cheap redemption. Senator X is sent to prison for some vicious and clearly-proven crime. He soon announces that he is now on personal terms with Jesus, and should therefore be let out early, and/or allowed to profit from selling the story of his felonies, and/or be allowed conjugal visits.

A very parallel fancy is that of rapid resolution of profound disagreements or injuries. Governor Y is exposed diverting a million dollars to his mistress who is also an illegal alien. The governor poses for the press with his grimly supportive wife and announces, "Let the healing begin." As this is being written, some memorial benches are dedicated outside the Pentagon, and the Washington *Post* announces that the families whose loved ones were butchered and incinerated by Muslim fanatics would find spiritual "comfort" in this outdoor furniture.

Such cheap pop psychology overlooks the Serbs, who are still bitter over losing the battle of Kosovo in 1448 A.D., or the Shias, who mourn the Hidden Imam, gone missing since 874 A.D. Closer to home, fragments of the Irish Republican Army still mourn the passing of their era of bloody bombings. Within the past year I have heard educated Southerners, in good suits, refer to the Civil War as "The War of Northern Aggression," and "Our Defense Against Northern Invasion." I recently was present at a Sons of Confederate Veterans meeting. Half the men refused to salute the Stars and Stripes or to recite the Pledge of Allegiance.

So, should we expect the passions of Dorence Atwater's life to have cooled by 1912, a mere two years after his death? Of course not. In the dark recesses of the human heart, bitterness has a half life longer than that of the most stable isotope. The brain may be New Testament, with forgiveness and turning the other cheek, but the heart is Old Testament, governed by a God of anger, wrath, and vengeance. A long memory and a quick temper.

The reader will recall that it was Samuel Breck who had Dorence tried, convicted, and shipped in manacles and chains to prison at hard labor. On August 13, 1912, George S. Goddard, librarian at the Connecticut State Library, wrote to Brig. Gen. Samuel Breck.

> Dear Sir: It may interest you to know that many of the most interesting papers, except the original Andersonville Death List, which I am told was destroyed in the San Francisco fire, gathered by the late Dorence Atwater, have been presented to the Connecticut State Library by his brother, Richard, to be known as "the Dorence Atwater Collection." Accompanying the collection are many notes related to Dorence Atwater's life and services made by his brother and clipped from various papers and official reports. Among these notes is a summary of the case of the court-martial proceedings just made by Dorence's brother, in which summary of the trial Richard has paid you a tribute and exonerated you in his judgment for the part which you officially took in the conviction of his brother. It occurred to me that you might be interested in this summary and might desire to add a statement of the trial as it now appears to you. If you are so interested and desire to make a historical statement related to the incident, which, of course, has been closed, I am willing to send you a copy of the summary by Dorence's brother Richard, which was received this morning.

Breck, retired by 1912, and living in Brookline, Massachusetts, wrote to the then current Judge Advocate General, E. H. Crowder. Breck enclosed Goddard's letter, "which will explain itself." Breck no longer had any records of the case and asked for a copy of the court-martial proceedings. "I will say in this connection that I do not feel the need of any exoneration [*I do not feel the need for any exoneration!* Author's interjection] as what I did was simply a part of my duty. I did not follow up Atwater after his sentence as he had been a prisoner at Andersonville, and it seemed to me that might fairly excuse a charitable view of his offense." On January 22, 1913, Gen. Breck sent his reply to Goddard.

Dear Sir I enclose herewith a copy of the proceedings of general court-martial by which Dorence Atwater was tried for taking certain records regarding Union prisoners in Andersonville Prison during the war of the Rebellion. The whole case is shown in these records and speaks for itself. Mr. Atwater has since died. Captain James M. Moore against whom Atwater's brother Richard makes his complaint, died April 25, 1905, holding the rank of Brigadier General on the retired list of the Army. I knew him well. He was a careful, faithful and honorable officer, and was very much displeased that Atwater should have taken the records while in his, Captain Moore's, custody. He so expressed himself to me. Of course, the enterprising newspaper correspondent made as interesting a report as he could on the information he obtained, but Captain Moore was not responsible for that. My recollection of the matter is that the example had been made and in view of Atwater's suffering as a prisoner in Andersonville Prison and the belief that he had been misled by trusted advisors, we were all rather pleased that the President had seen proper to remit a very considerable portion of his sentence. In my opinion, Mr. Richard Atwater's aspersions on Captain Moore and others are wholly unwarranted. Dorence Atwater and especially his unwise advisors are responsible for all his troubles. Very Respectfully Yours, Samuel Breck Brigadier General U.S.A. retired.

In the papers sent to Breck by Goddard, what so inflamed the old general? It was most likely the address that Francis Atwater had given at the Congregational Church at Terryville on May 29, 1911. The printed text runs twenty-two hundred words. Much of it rehearses the story described in earlier pages here. Francis added new and often crucial observations.

He [Dorence] persevered and by his forethought are preserved to the nation the names of thirteen hundred soldiers dead, who perished in Andersonville. Then comes the story of his trouble with the government, which had learned of his great work. At the time of his release from Andersonville, he had served twenty-two months since his capture. He came here to Terryville, a skeleton of his former self. He was taken down with diphtheria and lay at the point of death, but soon rallied, and before he had fully recuperated had been summoned to Washington. His precious rolls were demanded for government use, and while he was anxious to publish them for the benefit of relatives and friends of the Andersonville Victims, under threats of confiscation he consented his names should be copied. He then enlisted in the General Service, U.S.A., and was detailed as a clerk in one of the departments at Washington. The government had copied his rolls, but refused to return them. In July 1865, he informed Secretary [of War] Stanton that he could identify all of the graves at Andersonville if the work were undertaken immediately. The Secretary of War ordered the work performed, and detailed Captain Moore and forty others, including Dorence, to go to Andersonville at once. Included in the party was Clara Barton, one of the world's greatest benefactors. The original rolls were also taken. Headboards were erected to the thirteen thousand martyrs and the party returned. Shortly after, the rolls were missed. No one knew where they were, until Dorence was questioned, when he promptly answered he had taken his property where he could find it, which he said the law allowed a man to do. He was told he could have twenty-four hours to return his rolls, but he said he was determined to keep them. He was then and there arrested, placed in the Old Capitol Prison, was tried by court-martial and adjudged guilty, where upon he was sent to Auburn State Prison to serve at hard labor for eighteen months, fined three hundred dollars, and to stand committed until the rolls were returned. He possessed the old Kentish spirit of never being conquered. In irons he was taken from Washington to Auburn, where he served for two months, when he was discharged without the formality of a pardon. This [release] came about because Secretary Stanton feared General Ben Butler was about to start an investigation which was demanded by newspapers all over the country, the most persistent of which was the New York *Tribune.* Upon the release of Dorence his rolls were taken from their hiding place, put in alphabetical order, and twenty-five thousand copies printed by the Tribune Association and placed on the bookstands over the country before the government knew what was being done. He was now in his 21st year, broken down in health, a victim of both the South and the North, and although he had been cruelly and unjustly punished, so far as the government was concerned he was simply a discharged convict, released without the grace of a pardon. The government recognized this in a slight way by giving him a consulship in the far off Seychelles Islands.

In September 1910 Dorence telegraphed his brother, "Come at once if you wish to see me alive ..." Francis remembered their last meeting: "We had a splendid visit, so full of brotherly love and reminiscences. He was up and around ... and so I returned [to Connecticut]. He wrote me every few days ... the writing became more and more illegible, until the last letter which arrived the day he died, which was scarcely traceable ... He had a right to believe his course would receive the sanction of the government but instead to be brutally incarcerated at hard labor in state prison, was beyond his youthful comprehension. Do you wonder, years later, in one of his letters he should remark, 'The word soldier makes me mad, while the sight of a uniform makes me froth at the mouth.'"

A Summing Up

Even the longest and most convoluted story can have a key, sometimes a simple key, a central nidus, an inner core, around which all the rest is secondary. In my opinion that central core is summarized in the Gospel According to St. Matthew, Chapter 23, verses 23 and 24, in which the writer refers to a man who strains at a gnat and swallows a camel. This is the very leit-motif of obsessive-compulsive thinking, the inability to distinguish what is important from what is trivial.

Let me explain. Dorence emerged from the hells of Belle Isle, Smith's Tobacco Factory, Andersonville, and Florence, bearing his roster of the dead. His simple goal, his single goal, was to make these names available to the public, for the relief of families.

He never stated a wish for gratitude or for a medal, or for the equivalent of a photo op in the Oval Office. I believe his idea of a reward would have been in seeing the project completed. That was the camel.

The gnat was the creation of Samuel Breck. His focus was on procedure, on territory, on the power to control, and the power to obstruct. The letter of the law, but not the spirit of the law. At no juncture in the records of that forty-year saga did I see a single indication that Breck understood the purpose of Atwater's labor. Never once did Breck indicate that families missing a son, or a father, or a husband, or a lover, would find relief in knowing what happened to that missing soldier. Drew Gilpin Faust has pointed out that Victorian society had a well established and complex set of mourning rituals, but when the dead person was simply missing, these comforting acts were impossible. For Breck, the issue was not how to use the death list, but where to file it.

Some people find history dry and boring. What an error! What a sad error! As I read Dorence's treatment by the War Department, I wanted to shout, "That's not the main issue here! Stop everything! Give Dorence some money to treat his malaria and his diphtheria and to bury his father. Have your legion of copyists make a copy for your files and let Dorence take his copy to a newspaper, with an agreement that he not profit from it. Do not delay for a single day in bringing this news to twelve thousand grieving families. Forget the gnat; focus on the camel. Do you want credit for yourself? Fine. Call a press conference. Tell the reporters that you have realized the value of this list, that you have taken Dorence under your wing, that you will make sure it gets published — and soon. You could have been the hero. It could have been different, General Breck. You could have had your copy, made your little memoranda, quibbled inside your office about how to file it. You could have had it both ways, keeping control of one set while using Dorence to reflect well on you."

But, no. Just beyond my desk, in a shadowed corner, Breck's ghost pursed his thin lips. He stroked his perfectly trimmed beard. He stared down his nose at me. "Private Atwater defied me. I received disrespect. He defied the authority of the government. He was insubordinate to the Office of the Adjutant-General. He wanted this list to get rich. [What a way to get rich — lose eighty pounds in four prisons!] I was right and he was wrong. His time in prison? He asked for it!" Gnat and camel. Gnat and camel.

On December 3, 1919, in Connecticut, Francis Atwater testified, "There is absolutely no question that she is the legal widow of my brother Dorence Atwater." Two days later, Catherine Dikeman, a seventy year-old widow, told the deposer that her brother Dorence enlisted in the Army when he was sixteen. She was certain that this was the first and only marriage for both her brother and for Moetia. Dorence's commanders recalled his courage in combat. His compilation and successful concealment of the death list speaks for itself. *Res ipsa loquitor.* Bravery, loyalty, marital fidelity, steadfastness – all these counted for nothing in the dusty ledgers of the Adjutant-General.

Breck's ghost was fading now. Just a gray outline. I could see right through him. Then there was only the voice — "I was right and he was wrong. I was right. I was right." Then even the voice was gone. I had failed. I could not change history.

Things were as they were, and are as they are. When the game is over, pawns and kings go back in the same box. Atwater and Breck are both six feet under now. The reader may choose. Which man was the hero?

APPENDIX A

Clara Barton – A Complex Woman

Her story has been told at length in many excellent books, most recently those by Elizabeth Brown Pryor and Stephen B. Oates. The Atwater family has their own unique contribution. In a rare pamphlet, now in the library of SUNY Geneseo, Francis Atwater wrote of "Clara Barton Crucified by Designing Society Women of Washington."

He began by describing his visit to her on her ninetieth birthday, when she knew the end was drawing near. They talked about all her years of service, her career as a teacher, her services during the Civil War, the expedition to mark the Andersonville graves, her post-war bureau for missing soldiers, her role in the Franco-Prussian War, and her contribution to the Spanish-American War. Atwater described these episodes in great detail. After the Franco-Prussian war, she was so exhausted that she was confined to her home for years, but there was a benefit – her European sojourn put her in touch with the Red Cross movement and was a first step in founding the American Red Cross. Atwater reminded us of a long-ago event. After the Spanish surrendered at Santiago, Cuba, the first ship into the harbor was not a warship, but was the *State of Texas,* an unarmed freighter loaded with 1,400 tons of food for the Cuban people. Admiral Sampson put a pilot aboard the *Texas,* and with the flag of the Red Cross floating in the breeze, a banner not of triumph, crowing victory, but a pennant of goodwill and compassion, with this little lady on the bridge, the ship of mercy led the way.

Now, Francis Atwater's memories took on a more somber note. "The heartrending agony in her career came some eight years ago [1904] when she was sacrificed, yes crucified as ruthlessly as Jesus was on the cross, to satisfy the ambition of designing society women in Washington, who was abetted by the Imperial One [Theodore Roosevelt] ... the Red Cross was wrenched from her, and since then has been the plaything and football of the smart set in the capitol, headed by Miss Mabel Boardman. ... to prove that these pirates did not have any reason to put forth, but to cheap notoriety in deposing Miss Barton, I will state that Miss Boardman came to me at Meriden, knowing that I had great influence with Miss Barton, to ask my aid to have her accept the position of honorary president." Atwater continued at great length how, in his experience, Barton was "drawn and quartered" by the society ladies. The official American Red Cross web site has a photograph of Mabel Boardman. To me, her face is grim, challenging, combative. Even her official Red Cross biographical sketch notes that, "She was often considered overbearing." Maybe Atwater's impression was correct.

Although Barton never married or bore children, she seemed to have a capacity for romance. During her time at Hilton Head, she had an intense relationship with Col. John J. Elwell, a quartermaster, with a wife and children back in Ohio. At home, he was a professor of medical jurisprudence. He and Clara seemed to be philosophic and conversational soul mates. Unlike today, where sexual indiscretions are the grist of TV talk shows, Miss Barton's diary tells us – nothing. Perhaps that's as it should be.

A Minnesota Princess

Dorence and Moetia had no children, but their numerous Tahitian cousins, siblings, nieces, and nephews did reproduce. An article in the September 21, 1913 New York *Times* tells of one member of the Papara aristocracy who enrolled in a Minnesota public school in the late summer. The author, who lived through a winter in Minneapolis, with temperatures frequently below minus fourteen degrees Fahrenheit, could not help wondering what she thought of such weather, a shocking contrast with the tropics, where cascades of flowers and a plethora of mangoes, papayas, and coconuts greet each morning. The article tells us almost nothing of Princess Ina, but much about American's fascination with royalty – any royalty— and with Ina's brothers who <u>might</u> play football.

PRINCESS IN SCHOOL HERE—Royal Tahitian Maid Enrolls as a Pupil in Minneapolis. Princess Ina Salmon, a royal Tahitian maiden, has entered the public schools of Minneapolis, intending later to attend the State University. Past generations of her family have gone to England and Australia for their education, but if the Princess likes Minnesota her five brothers and one sister, all younger than she, will be American college graduates. Tutea Salmon, Princess Ina's eleven-year-old brother, and the eldest son of Tauraa Salmon, may some day be a star of the Minnesota football team. Speaking of him, Miss Josephine Tilden of St. Paul, who was largely instrumental in having the princess come to America, said: "Tutea is working hard in school at Tahiti, so that he may be able to come to Minnesota next year, his ambition being to play football and to be a cowboy. If he does come, he will win laurels on the athletic field, as there is no other race that shows such physical development as the Polynesian. And the Tahitians are the finest of these people. The young men of the island are learning to play football. Two English teams stopped there for several weeks last year, and the people went wild over the sport. Ina's father has a large cocoanut and vanilla plantation, and the Salmon family owns about half of the Island of Tahiti. Her grandfather, Chief Tati, has done much literary work. On a visit several years ago he spent a week as the guest of Col. [Theodore] Roosevelt. All his literary work, including a history of Tahiti, has been done in English."

APPENDIX C

Pacific Islanders in the Civil War

Not all Civil War soldiers and sailors were from the continental United States. The indefatigable Australian researcher, Terry Foenander (in conjunction with Ed Milligan), has combed thousand of obscure records and found hundreds of Asian and Oceanic servicemen. The full and more detailed roster can be viewed at http://www.tfoenander.com/asians.html. Ones relevant to Dorence Atwater's life are shown below. The island recorded is birthplace. The records cannot distinguish between Caucasian parents living in the islands and native islanders with Anglicized names. (Some records give skin, eye, and hair color.) The next entry is age, followed by unit or ship.

John Adams, Honolulu, Sandwich Islands (Hawaii), 23, 6th US Colored Troops.
Peter Adams, Sandwich Islands (Hawaii), 32, USS Clara Dolsen.
George Albert, Oahu, Sandwich Islands, 39, 5th Massachusetts Colored Cavalry.
William Allan, Mahe, Seychelles, 28, US Navy, ship not recorded.
Robert Andrews, "Polynesian," USS Black Hawk.
Auguste Aps, Mahe, Seychelles, 19, USS Pinola.
John Aram, Oahu, Sandwich Islands, 25, 5th Massachusetts Colored Cavalry
Charles Beeb, Tahiti, 35, US Navy, ship not recorded.
William Bill, Sandwich Islands (Hawaii), CSS Shenandoah.
John Boy, Sandwich Islands, (Hawaii), CSS Shenandoah.
Johnny Boy, Sandwich Islands, 22, USS Isonomia and USS San Jacinto.
John Brown, Honolulu, 22, 11th US Colored Heavy Artillery
John Brown, Friendly Islands (Tonga), 22, US Navy, ship not recorded.
James Bush, Sandwich Islands, 21, USS Vandalia and USS Beauregard.

William Brown, Sandwich Islands (Hawaii), CSS Shenandoah.

James California, Sandwich Islands (Hawaii), CSS Shenandoah.

James Crow, Friendly Islands (Tonga), 23, USS Sabine and USS Wabash.

Henry David, Sandwich Islands, 19, USS Vanderbilt.

Peter Davis, Oahu, Sandwich Islands, 26, 5th Massachusetts Colored Cavalry.

Howard Everson, Sandwich Islands, 21, 5th Massachusetts Colored Cavalry.

Mariano Flores, Honolulu, Sandwich Islands, 21, US Navy, ship not recorded.

Charles Foster, Society Islands (Tahiti), 22, 54th Massachusetts Infantry.

John Foster, Tahiti, 28, USS Albatross.

James French, Sandwich Islands (Hawaii), CSS Shenandoah.

John Franks, Oahu, Sandwich Islands, 25, 5th Massachusetts Colored Cavalry

Henry Givens, Sandwich Islands (Hawaii), CSS Shenandoah.

Elien Haley, Sandwich Islands, 26, USS San Jacinto.

John Hall, Sandwich Islands, 35, USS Ithasca.

Joseph Handy, "Decatur Island, South Pacific," 23, died at US Naval Hospital, Chelsea

John Hastings, Sandwich Islands, 28, USS Richmond and USS Estrella.

Charles Heatley, "Niyahu, Sandwich Islands," 26, 5th Massachusetts Colored Cavalry.

George Height, "S. Island," 32, USS Ohio and USS Colorado

George High, Sandwich Islands, 32, USS Vanderbilt.

George Holland, Sandwich Islands, 38, USS Lackawanna.

Henry Hollins, "Taluhana," 32, US Navy, ship not recorded.

Joseph Kanaca, Sandwich Islands (Hawaii), CSS Shenandoah.

Joseph Kanaka, Tahiti, 27, USS Potomac and USS Hartford.

Henry Lewis, Sandwich Islands, 30, USS Wateree.

Henry Lobson, Sandwich Islands, 25, USS Dacotah.

Joseph Long, Sandwich Islands (Hawaii), CSS Shenandoah.

John Mahoe, Sandwich Islands (Hawaii), CSS Shenandoah.

John Manuel, Sandwich Islands, 18, USS Vanderbilt.

Charles Newton, "Marquasar" (Marquesas?), 40, US Navy, ship not recorded.
John Ourai, Sandwich Islands, 23, US Navy, ship not recorded.
Antonio Perez, Honolulu. Sandwich Islands, 19, USS Wyoming.
Frederick Rain, Sandwich Islands, 30, USS Constellation.
William Rodoma, Sandwich Islands, 25, US Navy, ship not recorded.
Prince Romerson, Sandwich Islands (Hawaii), 24, 5th Massachusetts Colored Cavalry.
James Rontongo, Tahiti, 24, USS Potomac.
Joseph Rontongo, Tahiti, 27, US Navy, ship not recorded.
John Sailer, Sandwich Islands (Hawaii), CSS Shenandoah.
Benjamin Smart, "Pacific Islander, Navigator Island," 25, US Navy, ship not recorded.
Henry Smith, Sandwich Islands, 30, USS Hartford.
John Smith, "Friendly Islands (Tonga)," USS Monongahela.
John Smith, Oahu, Sandwich Islands, 25, USS Portsmouth.
Peter Smith, Oahu, Sandwich Islands, 27, USS Bohio.
Julius Stone, Sandwich Islands, 30, USS Ino.
Robert Tahiti, Tahiti, 29, USS George Maugham.
Isaac Thompson, Sandwich Islands, 19, USS Kennebec.
Peter Warren, Sandwich Islands, 30, USS Glaucus.
Samuel M. Watt, Sandwich Islands (Hawaii), 21, 20th US Colored Troops.
Henry Williams, Owhyhee [Oahu], Sandwich Islands, 31, USS Midnight.
James Williams, Tahiti, 27, US Navy, ship not recorded.

SOURCES

Chapter 1

Baldwin, Terry E.: "Clerk of the Dead – Dorence Atwater," *Civil War Times Illustrated*, Volume X, October 1971, pages 13–21.

Atwater, Francis: *Atwater History and Genealogy*, Volume 4, Horton Printing Co., Meriden, Connecticut, 1927.

Chapter 3

Marvel, William: *Andersonville: The Last Depot.* University of North Carolina Press, 1994.

Clothing Issued to Federal Prisoners. *Official Reports.* Series II, Volume VI, page 852.

Chapter 4

National Archives Record Group 153, Records of the Judge Advocate General's Office (Army), Entry 15, Case File MM2975. 8 boxes. (Wirz trial).

Chapter 5

Report of the Secretary of War, 1865. Pages 263–266.

Chapter 6

National Archives RG153, Case File MM2766. (Atwater trial).

Chapter 7

National Archives Record Group 59, General Records of the Department of State, Appointment Records, NARS A-1, Entry 778, Vol. 6 of 12, 250/48/02/01.

The complete Atwater death list has been reprinted and is available at the Eastern National bookstore at Andersonville National Historic Site.

Chapter 8

Dodd, Edward: *The Rape of Tahiti*. Dodd, Mead, New York, 1983.

O'Brien, Frederick: *Mystic Isles of the South Seas*. Century, New York, 1971.

O'Reilly, P.: *Les Tahitiens*. Publication de la Société des Océanistes, No. 36, Musée de l"Homme, Paris.

Adams, Henry: *Memoirs of Arii Taimai e Marama of Eimeo, Teriirere of Tooarai, Teriinui of Tahiti, Tauraatua i Amo*. 1901. (reprinted 1968, Gregg Press).

Chapter 9

Creighton, Margaret: *Rites and Passages*. Cambridge University Press, 1995.

Record of American and Foreign Shipping. American Shipmasters Association, New York, 1879.

Chapter 11

Civil War Pension File Wid. Orig. 1,061,830.

Chapter 12

Atwater, Francis: *Two Martyrs—Clara Barton and Dorence Atwater.* Privately printed, 1912.

Atwater, Francis: *History of the Town of Plymouth, with an Account of the Centennial Celebration, May 14 and 15, 1895.* (reprinted 1995.)

Faust, Drew Gilpin: "This is My Last Letter toYou." *Civil War Times,* February 2008, pages 28–35.

PHOTO CREDITS

Cover. Library of Congress, image #LC-USZ62-62748.

Older Dorence Atwater: SUNY Geneseo

Belle Isle Prison: Robert E. L. Krick collection.

Samuel Breck: US Army Military History Institute.

Hand-written letter: Court-martial of Dorence Atwater.

Cannon at Atwater Memorial: Plymouth Historical Society.

Funeral processions at Tahiti: Connecticut State Library.

Cruiser *Scharnhorst*: US Naval Historical Foundation.

Starved man: Library of Congress, image #LC-B8184-5526.

Made in the USA